CORE-PLUS MATHEMATICS PROJECT

Course
Part **B** **1**

Contemporary Mathematics in Context

A Unified Approach

CORE-PLUS MATHEMATICS PROJECT

Course 1

Part B

Contemporary Mathematics in Context

A Unified Approach

Arthur F. Coxford
James T. Fey
Christian R. Hirsch
Harold L. Schoen
Gail Burrill
Eric W. Hart
Ann E. Watkins
with
Mary Jo Messenger
Beth Ritsema

EVERYDAY LEARNING™

Chicago, Illinois

Cover images: Images © 1997 Photodisc, Inc.

Everyday Learning Development Staff

Editorial: Anna Belluomini, Eric Karnowski, Steve Mico

Production/Design: Fran Brown, Hector Cuadra, Michael Murphy, Jess Schaal, Norma Underwood, Marie Walz

Additional Credit: Michael Green

 This project was supported, in part, by the National Science Foundation.
The opinions expressed are those of the authors and not necessarily those of the Foundation.

ISBN 1-57039-478-4 (Part A)

ISBN 1-57039-482-2 (Part B)

Preface

Assessing what students know and are able to do is an integral part of the *Contemporary Mathematics in Context* curriculum. Opportunities for assessment occur in each phase of the instructional model, from the lesson launch discussions and follow-up investigations to the "Checkpoint" and "On Your Own" tasks. The MORE (Modeling, Organizing, Reflecting, and Extending) activities following the investigations provide another means for evaluating the level of understanding of each individual student. Methods for conducting these curriculum-embedded assessments include fundamental classroom techniques of observing, listening, and questioning. As the students work through each lesson, the teacher will have ample opportunity to observe and assess how the students think about and apply mathematics.

More formal assessment also can be made, and it is to that end that the materials in this resource book were created. For each unit, there are several different types of assessment activities presented here:

- Quizzes (two forms for each lesson)
- In-class exams (two forms for each unit)
- Take-home exam items (three for each unit)
- Projects (two for each unit)

Sample solutions are provided for the quizzes and in-class exams, and the take-home assessments include helpful teacher notes. Assessment tasks for a Midterm and a Final Exam are provided for *Contemporary Mathematics in Context*. For Part A of Course 1, the Midterm assessment tasks follow Unit 3. For Part B, a bank of Final assessment tasks follow Unit 7.

You also may want to refer to the *Contemporary Mathematics in Context Teacher's Guide*, which includes a valuable discussion of assessment and student evaluation. Among the topics presented are scoring assessments and assigning grades; both are topics of concern to all educators, especially to those who are implementing innovative teaching methods and mathematical content not typically taught in their classrooms.

Name _____   Date _____

Lesson 1 Quiz

Unit 5

1. The pictures below show two columns, one a circular cylinder and the other a square prism, that are made of the same type and amount of material.

   a. Which column type supports the most weight?

      Circular cylinder _____   *Square prism* _____

   b. Each of the space-shapes above has reflection symmetry. For example, a horizontal plane parallel to the bases of each figure and exactly halfway between the top and bottom is a plane of symmetry in each case. Describe and sketch two *vertical* planes of symmetry for each figure.

      Descriptions: *Sketches:*

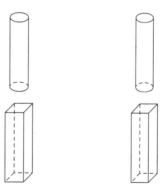

2. a. Sketch a prism and a pyramid, each of which has a base that is an equilateral triangle.

      Prism: *Pyramid:*

Lesson 1 Quiz

Unit 5

b. Is each space-shape in Part a rigid? If not, explain how to make it rigid.

Prism: Yes ____   No ____   *Pyramid: Yes ____   No ____*
Explanations if needed:

3. The following are three views of a cube model of a building.

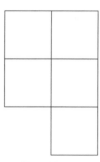   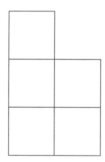   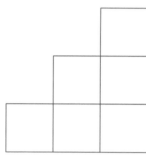

Top View   **Front View**   **Right Side View**

a. How tall (in stories) is the cube building? Explain how you can tell.

Height in stories: _____
Explanation:

b. Describe the location of the tallest part of the cube building. Explain how you arrived at your answer.

Description and explanation:

Suggested Solutions

1. **a.** The circular cylinder will support more weight than the prism.

   b. One vertical plane of symmetry for each figure is drawn below. In the circular cylinder, any plane through the segment joining the centers of the bases will work. In the square prism, the plane must contain two of the diagonals of the square bases, or contain the midpoints of opposite edges of the bases.

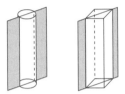

2. **a.** Prism: Pyramid:

   b. The pyramid is rigid. The prism is not, but it can be made rigid by inserting a diagonal in each of the rectangular faces.

3. **a.** Based on the front view or the right side view, you can tell the building has three stories. The top view tells you nothing about the height.

   b. The front view tells you that the tallest part is on the left side. The right side view tells you that the tallest part is in the back. Combining this information, it follows that the tallest part is in the back left corner.

Lesson 1 Quiz

Form B

1. **a.** Is this a sketch of a prism? Explain your reasoning.

    Yes ____ *No* ____
    Explanation:

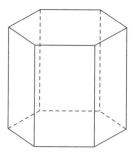

b. Is this the sketch of a rigid space-shape? If not, sketch in the minimum number of segments that will make it rigid.

Yes ____ *No* ____ *(Sketch any necessary segments on the figure above.)*

c. Sketch a pyramid that has a square base.

2. Does the following space-shape below have reflection symmetry? Explain your reasoning.

    Yes ____ *No* ____
    Explanation:

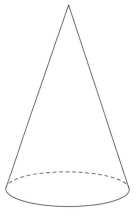

Use after page 354.

Lesson 1 Quiz

Unit 5

3. a. Sketch a straight-on front view of this cube model.

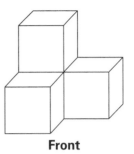

Front

b. Sketch a view from the right side.

c. Sketch a top view.

Suggested Solutions

1. **a.** Yes, it is a prism. The base is a polygon, in this case a hexagon, and the sides (faces) are rectangles.

    b. This is not a rigid space-shape. One way to make it rigid with a minimum number of supports is to triangulate both bases and each other rectangular face.

    c.

    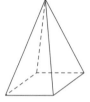

2. Yes. Any vertical plane that cuts the cone through the top vertex and the center of the circular base will cut it into identical mirror-image halves.

3. **a.**

    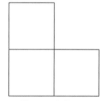

    Front View

    b.

    Right Side View

    c.

    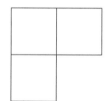

    Top View

Lesson 2 Quiz

Form A

1. On the grid below, sketch two rectangles that have equal areas but different perimeters. Label one rectangle I and the other II. Find the perimeters and areas of each rectangle. Show or explain your work in each case.

Sketches: *Work or explanation:*

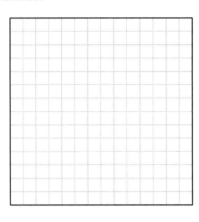

Rectangle I: *Area:* _____   *Perimeter:* _____

Rectangle II: *Area:* _____   *Perimeter:* _____

2. One leg of a right triangle is 12 cm and the hypotenuse is 22 cm. Use your calculator to find the length of the other leg to the nearest tenth of a centimeter. Write out the calculations that you entered on your calculator.

Length of other leg: _____
Description of calculations:

Lesson 2 Quiz

3. **a.** Boxes in the shape of prisms with square bases are used to ship hammers. The base of each box is 5 inches on a side, and the height is 14 inches. Sketch a box below and label its dimensions.

Sketch of a box with dimensions labeled:

b. Find the volume of a box with dimensions described in Part a. Show or explain your work. Be sure to write the appropriate units for the volume.

Volume: _____

Work or explanation:

Unit 5

Suggested Solutions

1. Responses will vary. Two possible rectangles are shown below.

Rectangle I
Area: 36 units^2
Perimeter: 26 units

Rectangle II
Area: 36 units^2
Perimeter: 24 units

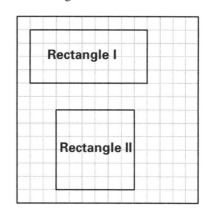

2. The length of the other leg, to the nearest tenth, is 18.4 cm. Using the Pythagorean Theorem, the length of the missing leg can be found by calculating $\sqrt{22^2 - 12^2}$.

3. **a.**

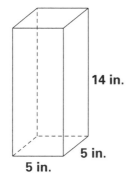

14 in.

5 in.

5 in.

b. V = length $\times$ width $\times$ height = $(5)(5)(14)$ = 350 cubic inches.

Lesson 2 Quiz

Form B

1. On the grid below, sketch two rectangles that have equal perimeters but different areas. Label one rectangle I and the other II. Find the perimeters and areas of each rectangle. Show or explain your work in each case.

    Sketches: *Work or explanation:*

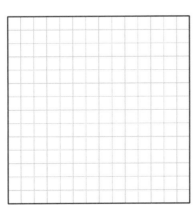

    Rectangle I: *Perimeter:* _____   *Area:* _____

    Rectangle II: *Perimeter:* _____   *Area:* _____

2. One leg of a right triangle is 15 cm and the hypotenuse is 24 cm. Use a calculator to find the length of the other leg to the nearest tenth of a centimeter. Write out the calculations that you entered on your calculator.

    Length of other leg: _____
    Description of calculations:

Lesson 2 Quiz

3. a. A beverage company packages bottles of apple cider in gift boxes. The boxes are in the shape of prisms with square bases. The base of each box is 6 inches on a side and the height is 13 inches. Sketch a box and label its dimensions.

b. One of the gift boxes in Part a is to be wrapped. What is the area that must be covered with wrapping paper? Show or explain your work. Be sure to write the appropriate unit for the area.

Area: _____

Work or explanation:

Suggested Solutions

1. Responses will vary. Two possible rectangles are shown below.

Rectangle I
Perimiter: 24 units
Area: 32 units^2

Rectangle II
Perimeter: 24 units
Area: 36 units^2

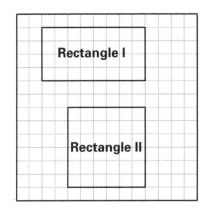

2. The length of the other leg, to the nearest tenth, is 18.7 cm. Using the Pythagorean Theorem, the length of the missing leg can be found by calculating $\sqrt{24^2 - 15^2}$.

3. **a.**

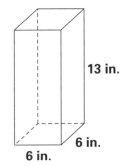

13 in.

6 in.

6 in.

b. All faces must be covered with wrapping paper. The top and the bottom each have area (6)(6) or 36 square inches. The vertical faces are all 6 × 13 rectangles, so each face has an area of 78 square inches. The total area that must be covered with wrapping paper is (2)(36) + (4)(78) or 384 square inches.

Use after page 382.

Lesson 3 Quiz

1. **a.** Sketch a plane-shape that is a polygon and another that has line segments for sides but is not a polygon.

   Polygon: *Not a polygon:*

   b. Describe the characteristics or properties of a plane-shape that make it a polygon.

2. Sketch a plane-shape that has rotational symmetry but not line (or reflection) symmetry.

Unit 5

Lesson 3 Quiz

Unit 5

3. Can this six-square pattern be folded into a cube? Explain your reasoning.

Yes ____   *No* ____
Explanation:

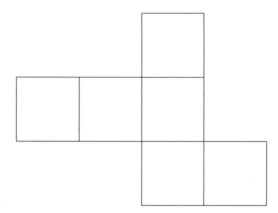

4. Describe the symmetries of this strip pattern. Think of it as continuing indefinitely to the right and the left in this pattern.

Description of symmetries:

Suggested Solutions

1. **a.** There are infinitely many possibilities for polygons, such as the following.

Examples of non-polygons are the following:

   b. Some characteristics of polygons are the following:

   ■ Each side intersects exactly two others, one at each of its endpoints.

   ■ The plane-shape is closed (no side is left unconnected at either endpoint).

   ■ Sides do not overlap other sides except at endpoints.

   ■ All of the sides are in the same plane (flat surface).

2. Responses will vary. A plane-shape has rotational symmetry if you can turn a copy of it and "fit it" onto the original. Below is an example.

3. Yes. A verbal description or a picture marked as below may be given.

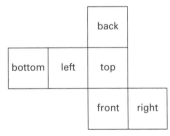

4. The given strip pattern has vertical line symmetry, translational symmetry, and glide reflection symmetry. Line symmetry is about a vertical line through the center of any polygon in the pattern. Sliding the entire pattern two (or any even number of) polygons to the right or left shows translational symmetry. Sliding the entire pattern one polygon (or any odd number of polygons) to the right or left, followed by a reflection across a horizontal line through the midpoints of vertical sides of the polygons, shows the glide reflection symmetry.

Lesson 3 Quiz

Form B

1. **a.** Is the following plane-shape a polygon? Explain your reasoning.

    Yes ____ *No* ____

    Explanation:

    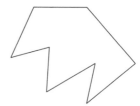

    b. Describe the characteristics or properties of a plane-shape that make it a polygon.

2. Sketch a plane-shape that has rotational and line (reflection) symmetry. Draw in all lines of symmetry, and describe the angle(s) of rotation.

Use after page 415.

Lesson 3 Quiz

3. Can this six-square pattern be folded into a cube? Explain your reasoning.

Yes _____ *No* _____
Explanation:

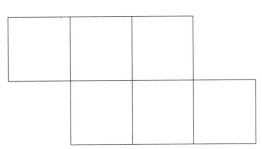

Unit 5

4. Describe the symmetries of this strip pattern. Think of it as continuing indefinitely to the right and the left in this pattern.

Description of symmetries:

Suggested Solutions

1. **a.** Yes, because the figure has the defining characteristics of a polygon as given in part b below.

   b. Some characteristics of polygons are the following:

   ■ Each side intersects exactly two others, one at each of its endpoints.

   ■ The plane-shape is closed (there is no side not connected at both endpoints).

   ■ Sides do not overlap other sides except at endpoints.

   ■ All of the sides are in the same plane (flat surface).

2. Responses will vary. There are many examples, including those shown below. Lines of symmetry are shown. The figure on the left can be rotated through 180°, clockwise or counterclockwise. The figure on the right can be rotated through 90°, 180°, and 270°, in either the clockwise or counterclockwise direction.

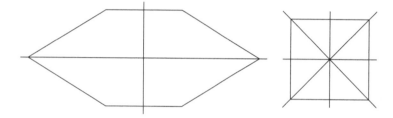

3. No. The portion where four squares meet at a vertex cannot be manipulated to form a cube without making cuts. You cannot get a single square for a face on each of the six sides.

4. The given strip pattern has reflection symmetry, translational symmetry, and glide reflection symmetry. There is reflection symmetry about any line that contains the long part of any arrow. Slide the strip two (or any even number) of arrows to the right (or left) to see the translational symmetry. For the glide reflection, slide the strip one arrow (or any odd number of arrows) to the right (or left), and then reflect it across the horizontal line that bisects the strip.

In-Class Exam

1. The following scale drawing of Land's End Lake, a popular vacation spot, is covered with a grid of squares. Each side of each small square represents 10 meters.

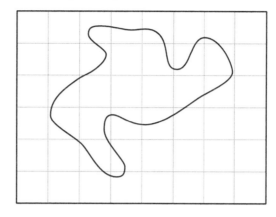

   a. On their vacation, Seth and Carol hiked all the way around the edge of Land's End Lake. Explain how you would estimate the distance that they hiked.

   Explanation:

   b. The developers of Land's End Lake would like to allow motorboats on the lake. For a small motor permit, the state requires that a lake cover at least 1,500 square meters. Explain how you would estimate the area of Land's End Lake.

   Explanation:

In-Class Exam

Unit 5

2. Describe all symmetries of each of the plane-shapes and the strip pattern sketched below. If the figure has line symmetry, draw or describe all lines of symmetry. If it has rotational symmetry, identify the center and angle(s) of rotation. If it has translational or glide reflection symmetry, describe that.

Descriptions of symmetries:

a.

b.

c.

d. Think of this strip pattern as continuing indefinitely in both directions.

Use after page 418.

In-Class Exam

Form A

3. Some regular polygons can be used as a basic pattern to tile, or cover, the plane; others cannot.

   a. List three regular polygons, each with a different number of sides, that can be used to tile the plane.

   1.

   2.

   3.

   b. Write a rule for how to tell whether a given regular polygon can be used to cover the plane. Explain why your rule is correct.

   Rule:

   Explanation:

4. The net below is for a space-shape.

   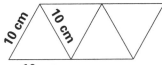

   10 cm

   a. Name the space-shape for which this is a net.

In-Class Exam

Unit 5

b. Make a three-dimensional drawing of the space-shape, with the hidden edges represented by dotted lines.

c. Find the surface area of the space-shape. Be sure to state your unit of measure.

Unit 5

Suggested Solutions

1. **a.** Responses may vary. One method is to place a string along the perimeter of the drawing, and then measure the length of the string. Another method that uses the grid is to estimate the length of the lake's edge that is in each 10 m by 10 m square, and then add those estimates. There are many other ways to estimate the lake's perimeter, of course.

    b. By estimating the fractional parts of squares that are filled and adding the 100 square meters for each square entirely included in the lake, you can find an estimate of the area. This is a case where a fairly accurate estimate is needed.

2. **a.** This figure has rotational symmetry. The center of rotation is the point of intersection of the diagonals, and the angle is 180°.

    b. This figure has three lines of symmetry, *p*, *q*, and *r*, shown below. It also has rotational symmetry centered at the point of intersection of the three lines of symmetry. The possible angles of rotation are 120° and 240° in either the clockwise or counterclockwise direction.

    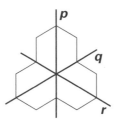

    c. This figure is symmetric about each of the lines containing double arrows and the two lines drawn in on the figure at the right. It also has rotational symmetry about the point of intersection of these lines through angles of 90°, 180°, and 270° in either the clockwise or counterclockwise direction.

    d. This strip pattern has translational symmetry. Any black dot may be translated to any other black dot. It also has horizontal line symmetry over the line containing the points.

3. **a.** (1) a regular, or equilateral, triangle

    (2) a square (regular quadrilateral)

    (3) a regular hexagon

    b. A rule that applies here is that the measure of the vertex angle of the polygon must be a divisor of 360. In the case of the regular triangle, 60° is a divisor of 360°; 90° is a divisor of 360° for the square; and 120° is a divisor of 360° for the regular hexagon. If the measure of the angle did not divide 360, it would be impossible to place the figures together without any overlaps or gaps.

Suggested Solutions *(continued)*

4. a. This is a tetrahedron net.

b.

c. If h is the slant height, then $h = \sqrt{10^2 - 5^2}$
or approximately 8.66 cm.

$$SA \approx \frac{1}{2}(10)(8.66)(4)$$

$$SA \approx 173.2 \text{ cm}^2$$

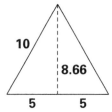

An alternative solution method would be to find the area of the parallelogram-shaped net.
The parallelogram has height approximately 8.66 and length 20. So the area is approximately
20(8.66) or 173.2 cm².

In-Class Exam

1. The following scale drawing of Otter Lake, a popular fishing spot, is covered with a grid of squares. Each side of each small square represents 10 meters.

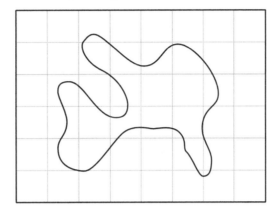

a. One beautiful day, Tina and her father rowed around the outer edge of Otter Lake, stopping to fish for a while at promising spots near the shore. Explain how you might estimate the total distance they rowed.

   Explanation:

b. Explain how you would estimate the area of Otter Lake.

   Explanation:

2. Describe all the symmetries of each of these figures. If the figure has line symmetry, draw or describe all lines of symmetry. If it has rotational symmetry, identify the center and angle of rotation. If it has translational or glide reflection symmetry, describe that.

Descriptions of symmetries:

a.

b.

c.

d. Think of the strip pattern as continuing
indefinitely in both directions.

Use after page 418.

In-Class Exam

3. Sketch three polygons that tile the plane: a triangle, a quadrilateral, and a hexagon. Explain whether each polygon is or is not a rigid plane-shape. If it is not, describe how it could be made rigid using the smallest number of supports.

   a. *Sketch of triangle:*   *Rigid? Yes* ____ *No* ____

   Explanation:

   b. *Sketch of quadrilateral:*   *Rigid? Yes* ____ *No* ____

   Explanation:

   c. *Sketch of hexagon:*   *Rigid? Yes* ____ *No* ____

   Explanation:

In-Class Exam

4. The net below is for a space-shape.

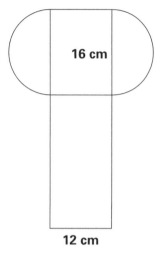

16 cm

12 cm

a. Name the space-shape for which this is a net.

b. Make a three-dimensional drawing of the space-shape with the hidden edges represented by dotted lines.

c. Find the volume of the space-shape. Be sure to state your unit of measure.

Suggested Solutions

1. **a.** Responses may vary. One method is to place a string along the perimeter of the lake, and then measure the length of the string. Another method that uses the grid is to estimate the length of the lake's edge that is in each 10 m by 10 m square, and then add those estimates. There are many other ways to estimate the lake's perimeter, of course.

    b. By estimating the fractional parts of squares that are filled, and adding the 100 square meters for each square entirely included in the lake, you can find an estimate of the area. Some students may estimate the area in another way. In general, if the estimation strategy makes sense and is completed in a reasonably accurate manner, give the student credit.

2. **a.** This figure is a rhombus; that is, the four sides have the same length. It is symmetric about either of its diagonal lines. It also has rotational symmetry about the point of intersection of its diagonals through angles of 180° in either the clockwise or counterclockwise direction.

    b. This figure has rotational symmetry about the point marked O through angles of 120° or 240° in either the clockwise or counterclockwise direction.

    c. This figure is symmetric about each of the lines containing the segments between the double arrows and the two lines drawn on the figure at the right. It also has rotational symmetry about the point of intersection of the arrowed segments through angles of 90°, 180°, and 270° in either the clockwise or counterclockwise direction.

    d. This strip pattern has horizontal, translational, and glide reflection symmetry. The horizontal symmetry is about the line containing the dots. The translational symmetry can be seen by sliding the pattern either to the right or left the distance between two consecutive darkened circles. (In fact, the distance between any two darkened circles could be used. The circles need not be consecutive.) The glide reflection symmetry can be seen by following one of the translations described above with a reflection in the horizontal mid-line of the pattern.

Unit 5

Suggested Solutions *(continued)*

3. **a.** Any triangle tiles the plane and is a rigid plane figure.

    b. Any quadrilateral tiles the plane. It is not rigid, but the figure resulting from adding a diagonal to a quadrilateral is rigid.

    c. A regular hexagon will tile the plane. As is the case for quadrilaterals and pentagons, the figure resulting from drawing all (in this case, three) diagonals from one vertex is a rigid plane-figure.

4. **a.** This would be the half of a cylinder formed by slicing through the diameters of the circular top and bottom of the cylinder. Students may choose to call this a "half-cylinder" or "semi-cylinder."

    b.

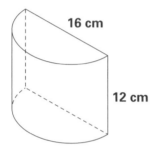

16 cm

12 cm

    c. V = area of the semicircle × height of the cylinder

    $$V = \frac{1}{2}(8^2\pi)(12)$$

    $$V \approx 1206 \text{ cm}^3$$

Take-Home Assessment

1. Develop a short lesson that you can give to an art class on the different kinds of space-shapes and patterns discussed in this unit. The goal of your lesson is to enable your students to identify the different kinds of space-shapes and plane patterns in various artwork from different cultures. Your lesson should include the following: an easy-to-understand explanation of the kinds of symmetry and other patterns discussed in Unit 5; some tasks that your students can complete so you can check their understanding of your explanations; and some artwork (at least pictures of it) from different cultures to test how well your students can apply what they have learned. If possible, try your lesson with some students who have not studied this unit and report on how it went, what worked well, and what should be revised.

2. Write an essay test for this unit. Your test should require your classmates to answer any three of four essay questions in a 50-minute period. Together the questions should cover all the main ideas in the unit. The questions should be structured so that enough information is required to be sure that good answers will reflect an understanding of these main ideas. After writing each question, write a sample answer that you think would deserve an "excellent" rating. Finally, suggest a way to score the answers to each problem, giving some credit for partially correct responses. Your scores on each question should range from an "excellent" response to no response at all. Have at least four ratings (such as 0, 1, 2, or 3 points) for each question, and briefly justify your thinking behind each score.

3. Suppose your school administrators are planning to improve the interior and exterior of the school building by painting designs in various places (above lockers, over doorways, above chalkboards, around the gym, and so forth). They also plan to include a new piece of sculpture for the main entrance. You are in charge of providing student input to the administration concerning these improvements. To do this, you are to develop two different designs for the artwork and sculpture. You must submit a written description of each design which discusses the main features in terms of a central theme and the symmetry, shape, and form of each paint design and the sculpture. Finally, you need to discuss which designs are better in terms of costs and labor for putting them in the building. For example, a design that is too complicated is probably too labor intensive, or a design that has large colored patterns may require too much paint. Include all these considerations in your written recommendations to the school administrators.

1. Projects like this one are based on research on learning which shows a clear increase in understanding of content when the learner attempts to teach it to someone else. The process of thinking carefully about how others may learn particular ideas, or have difficulty learning those ideas, helps to clarify these ideas in the mind of the teacher. This kind of activity should also provide you, the teacher of the "student teacher," with a good opportunity to observe what your students understand about the material, what they see as the difficulties, and how they would organize their thinking about the content so that someone else could understand it as they do. Following through and having the students teach their lessons is not necessary, but if it can be arranged the experience is another opportunity for significant learning to take place.

2. This is a high-level assignment that would, as you know, be difficult for anyone to do well. It offers much of the same learning opportunities for your students and assessment opportunities for you that are described in Task 1 above. In this case, it is especially important that you give students feedback at least once followed by a chance to revise their test. It would also be a good learning experience if other students had a chance to react to student-written tests.

3. This is a project that should be done by students working in pairs or small groups. It would be best if your school administration really was planning some improvements along the lines described in the project description. If another real-life opportunity like this presents itself in your community or neighborhood, the setting could be switched. For example, a student's parents may be building a house or doing major remodeling, or a business or community government building may be under construction or remodeling. The added realism of studying an ongoing building improvement project may be worth having students conduct this assessment outside the school setting.

Use after page 418.

Project

Geometry, Geometry Everywhere

Purpose

Geometry provides the language and concepts to describe the appearance, shape, size, and patterns of objects in the real world. For this project you will have to take notice of geometry in your own surroundings, thereby helping you to better understand, appreciate, and communicate the ideas of geometry.

Directions

1. Some of the main ideas in this unit are symmetry, measures (such as area, perimeter, and volume), tessellations, and rigidity. Find in your community one or more interesting examples of buildings, bridges, plane patterns (such as park designs, designs in nature, or even designs in wallpaper), or other objects or structures which can be described using these important geometric ideas.

2. Choose your example or examples so that when you write descriptions of them, you will make use of all four of the main geometric ideas given above at least once. This means that you may find one example whose description involves all four of the ideas. For example, the super-structure of a large building that is under construction may have various symmetries, some patterns in it you could describe as tessellations, and some area or perimeter measures and rigidity properties that may be important features to describe. On the other hand, it may be difficult to find just one example that makes use of all four geometric ideas in its description. In that case, find a second or third example and write a description of each of them.

3. Make photographs or sketches of your examples that illustrate the geometric ideas in your descriptions.

4. Organize the written descriptions and visual material to make an attractive poster illustrating "geometry in the real world" for display on the bulletin board in your classroom or for parent meetings.

Unit 5

Geometry, Geometry Everywhere

This project is probably best done by pairs or small groups of students working together. Their discussions before, during, and after the project should be valuable learning activities. Perhaps different students in a group could focus on different geometric ideas initially and then merge their efforts in the final poster.

Suggested Timeline

Allow students at least a day or two to find examples in the community and get feedback from you about whether the examples are appropriate. Two deadlines will be helpful, one for submitting some sketches and photographs with a rough design for the poster to which you provide feedback. The second deadline would be for submitting the poster in its final form. Students should have at least a week to submit the draft material and at least a week after that for the final poster.

Suggested Poster Guidelines

You may have a format that you would like students to use. If not, try the following:

- Written and visual material for each of the four geometric ideas assigned
- Well-organized poster display with an appropriate title and attractive use of color

Suggested Evaluation Criteria

Inform the students of your criteria at the time that you make the assignment. A sample breakdown is given here.

1. Work done on time   10%
2. Format of the poster follows directions   10%
3. Appropriate examples of all four geometric ideas   30%
4. Clarity and accuracy of written descriptions and sketches   30%
5. Poster quality (attractive and communicates its message well) 20%

Project

WOW! MOM + DAD

Purpose

Symmetry is an idea in mathematics that has practical applications to fields like art, architecture, construction, and mechanics. This project involves a much less practical, but interesting, use of symmetry; namely, the symmetry of printed words. This topic has long been a popular recreation, perhaps because it is a simple connection between the literary and the mathematical.

Directions

1. A *palindrome* is a word that is spelled the same forward or backward such as madam. Compile a list of at least ten palindromes. (**Hint:** Notice the words in the title of this project.)

2. Check each of the ten palindromes for all of the types of symmetry discussed in Unit 5. Feel free to use letter types that provide the most symmetry. Write a brief description of the symmetry of each of your palindromes.

3. Put your palindromes into categories in which two palindromes are in the same category if they exhibit exactly the same kinds of symmetry.

4. Compile a list of other words that have some sort of symmetry but are not palindromes, such as *pod*. You may include words, letters, phrases, or symbols from other cultures and languages.

5. Check each of your words for all of the types of symmetry discussed in Unit 5. Again, feel free to use letter types that provide the most symmetry. Write a brief description of the symmetry of each of your words.

6. Write a general description of the characteristics of a word that falls into each category based on its symmetries.

Unit 5

WOW! MOM + DAD

Students should have fun trying to generate these lists of words in groups. Be prepared for some words that may have offensive or off-color meanings. After some time for open searching, students should begin to look for general rules for words with particular symmetries. This will require focusing on the symmetries of letters. The type faces used for letters can limit their symmetries; hence, they can limit the symmetries of words formed by the letters. Have students use the most symmetric form of a particular letter. Some examples are shown below.

A H W O Z

Suggested Timeline

This project can probably best be done in small groups over a two- or three-day period. After reading the assignment on the first day, groups could spend ten minutes or so generating words that satisfy the required descriptions. For homework, each student could look for more words. On the second day, each group could compile their lists and discuss the symmetries of each word. For homework, students could be directed to begin to think about general rules for words in each category of symmetry.

Report Format

A suggested format is given here.

- Ten palindromes with a brief discussion of the symmetries of each
- Other words (perhaps five or more) with a brief discussion of the symmetries of each
- Categories of words which have the same symmetries
- A description of the general characteristics of words in each category

Suggested Evaluation Criteria

Inform the student of your criteria at the time that you make the assignment. A sample breakdown is given here.

1. Work done on time	10%
2. Format of the report follows directions	10%
3. Accuracy of the symmetries for each word	25%
4. Accuracy of the categories according to symmetries	25%
5. Accuracy and completeness of the general category descriptions	30%

Lesson 1 Quiz

1. A particular one-celled animal divides into two identical animals every 30 minutes.

    a. If 10 of these animals are present in a sample now, how many will be present after 60 minutes (assuming none of them die)? Show or explain your work.

    Number present: _____

    b. Write a *NOW-NEXT* equation that can be used to calculate the number of animals present after any number of 30-minute periods.

    NEXT = _____

    c. Write a rule that includes exponents and begins "*y* = …" that can be used to calculate the number of animals present after any number of 30-minute periods.

    y = _____

    d. Use the rules from Parts b and c to complete the following table:

Number of 30-minute Time Periods	0	1	2	3	4	5
Number of Animals Present						

    e. How many animals will be present in the sample after 5 hours? Explain.

    Number present: _____

    Explanation:

Unit 6

Lesson 1 Quiz

Form A

2. Calculate 3^7 without using the exponent key ($\boxed{\wedge}$ or $\boxed{y^x}$) on your calculator. Explain how you did it.

Answer: _____

Explanation:

3. Consider the pattern produced by the rule $y = 1.5^x$.

   a. Make a table of (x, y) values, finding y to the nearest tenth, for x from 0 to 10 in steps of 1.

x	0	1	2	3	4	5	6	7	8	9	10
y											

   b. Mark an appropriate scale on the y-axis below. Plot the points from your table in Part a.

   c. Describe the way that y changes as x increases.

   Description:

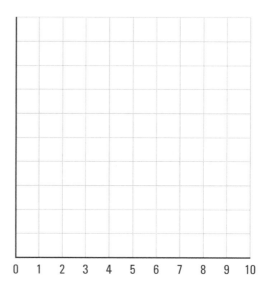

Suggested Solutions

1. **a.** There would be 40 animals after 60 minutes. After 30 minutes, there are $2 \times 10 = 20$, and after 60 minutes there are $2 \times 20 = 40$.

    b. $NEXT = 2 \times NOW$, starting with 10

    c. $y = 10(2)^x$

    d.

Number of 30-minute Time Periods	0	1	2	3	4	5
Number of Animals Present	10	20	40	80	160	320

    e. There will be 10,240 animals present after 5 hours, since 5 hours is ten 30-minute time periods. Use the formula $y = 10(2)^{10}$.

2. The answer is 2,187. An easy way to find this is to enter the following:
    3 [×] 3 [ENTER] [×] 3 [ENTER] [ENTER] [ENTER] [ENTER] [ENTER]

3. **a.**

x	0	1	2	3	4	5	6	7	8	9	10
y	1	1.5	2.3	3.4	5.1	7.6	11.4	17.1	25.6	38.4	57.7

    b.

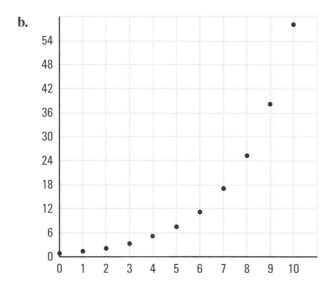

    c. As x increases, y increases at an increasing rate. For every unit increase in x, y is multiplied by 1.5. The equation $NEXT = 1.5 \times NOW$ fits this situation.

Lesson 1 Quiz

Form B

1. Suppose your school wants to hire you for 13 days of painting in the summer. You are to choose between two payment plans. With Plan 1, you would be paid $25 per day. With Plan 2, you would be paid 10¢ for accepting the job. Then your pay would be 20¢ for the first day, 40¢ for the second day, and so on, for the 13 days of work.

   a. How much would your total pay for 13 days be if you chose Plan 1. Explain or show your work.

   Total pay: _____

   Explanation:

   b. Complete the following table for Plan 2.

Day Number	0	1	2	3	4	5	6
Amount Earned	0.10	0.20	0.40				

Day Number	7	8	9	10	11	12	13
Amount Earned							

   c. Based on your answers to Parts a and b, with which plan would you be paid more money for these 13 days of work?

   d. Write a *NOW-NEXT* equation that can be used to calculate each day's earnings under Plan 2.

   NEXT = _____

   e. Write a rule beginning "$y = ...$" that can be used to calculate each day's earnings under Plan 2.

   $y =$ _____

Use after page 438.

2. Calculate 5^8 without using the exponent key ($\boxed{\wedge}$ or $\boxed{y^x}$) on your calculator. Explain how you did it.

Answer: _____

Explanation:

3. Consider the pattern produced by the rule $y = 1.3^x$.

    a. Make a table of (x, y) values, finding y to the nearest tenth, for x from 0 to 10 in steps of 1.

x	0	1	2	3	4	5	6	7	8	9	10
y											

    b. Mark an appropriate scale on the y-axis below. Plot the points from your table in Part a.

    c. Describe the way that y changes as x increases.

    Description:

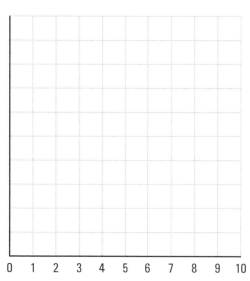

Unit 6

Suggested Solutions

1. **a.** $325. You would earn $13 \times \$25$.

   b.

Day Number	0	1	2	3	4	5	6
Amount Earned	0.10	0.20	0.40	0.80	1.60	3.20	6.40

Day Number	7	8	9	10	11	12	13
Amount Earned	12.80	25.60	51.20	102.40	204.80	409.60	819.20

   c. Under Plan 2 you would make more money.

   d. $NEXT = 2 \times NOW$, starting with 0.10

   e. $y = 0.10(2)^x$

2. The answer is 390,625. An easy way to find this is to enter

   5 $\boxed{\times}$ 5 $\boxed{\text{ENTER}}$ $\boxed{\times}$ 5 $\boxed{\text{ENTER}}$ $\boxed{\text{ENTER}}$ $\boxed{\text{ENTER}}$ $\boxed{\text{ENTER}}$

3. **a.**

x	0	1	2	3	4	5	6	7	8	9	10
y	1	1.3	1.7	2.2	2.9	3.7	4.8	6.3	8.2	10.6	13.8

   b.

   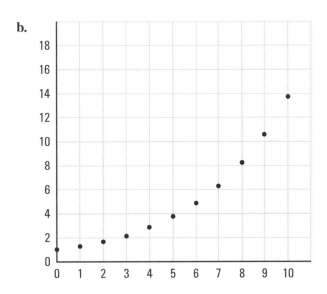

   c. As x increases, y increases at an increasing rate. For each unit increase in x, y is multiplied by 1.3. The equation $NEXT = 1.3 \times NOW$ describes this pattern.

Use after page 438.

Lesson 2 Quiz

1. Two exponential growth and decay situations are represented by graphs (1) and (2) and also by tables (A) and (B). For each graph there is a matching table.

    a. Write the number of the graph beside its corresponding table.

    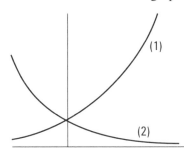

    _____ (A)

x	1	2	3	4
y	6	12	24	48

    _____ (B)

x	1	2	3	4
y	1.5	0.75	0.375	0.1875

    b. The equation of graph (1) in Part a is of the form $y = a(b)^x$. Will b be less than 1 or greater than 1? Explain your answer.

    Greater ____   *Less* ____

    Explanation:

2. Coffee, tea, and some soft drinks contain the drug caffeine. One hour after ingestion, 75% of the original amount of caffeine remains. At the end of each hour after that, 75% of the amount at the beginning of the hour remains. Suppose a person consumes 40 milligrams of caffeine.

    a. How much of that 40 milligrams (mg) will remain after 1, 2, and 3 hours?

    1 hour: ____   *2 hours:* ____   *3 hours:* ____

    b. Write a *NOW-NEXT* equation that can be used to calculate the amount of caffeine that will remain after any number of hours.

    NEXT = _____

c. Write a rule beginning *"y = ..."* that can be used to calculate the amount of caffeine that will remain *x* hours after the initial dose.

$y =$ _____

d. Use the equations from Parts b or c to make a table showing the amount of caffeine left at 1-hour intervals for 0 to 5 hours.

Number of Hours	0	1	2	3	4	5
Caffeine (mg)	40					

e. Make a plot of the data from Part d, and then a continuous graph of your *"y = ..."* rule. Use your calculator (or computer software), then copy the plot and graph below.

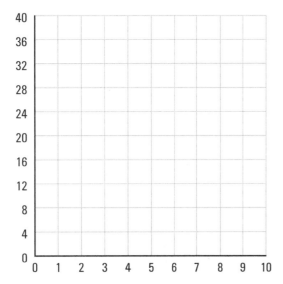

f. How long will it take for less than 1 milligram of caffeine to remain? Explain or show your work.

Time required: _____

Explanation:

Suggested Solutions

1. **a.** Graph (1) matches table (B); graph (2) matches table (A).

    b. The graph decreases as x increases, so the base must be less than 1. A base less than 1 raised to increasing positive powers causes the y values to decrease.

2. **a.** There will be 30 mg, 22.5 mg, and 16.9 mg after 1, 2, and 3 hours, respectively.

    b. $NEXT = 0.75 \times NOW$, starting with 40

    c. $y = 40(0.75)^x$

    d.

Number of Hours	0	1	2	3	4	5
Caffeine (mg)	40	30	22.5	16.9	12.7	9.5

    e.

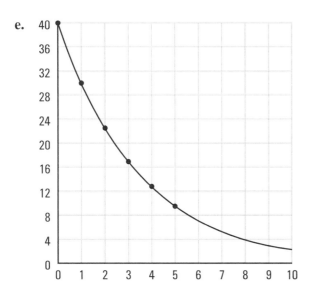

    f. It will take 13 hours for the amount of caffeine to be less than 1 mg. One way to find this is to use the exponential key and trial and error. Another way is to enter 40 ⨯ 0.75 [ENTER] ⨯ 0.75 [ENTER], then repeatedly press [ENTER] until the response is less than 1. In each approach, the value is less than 1 for the first time when the exponent is 13. Students also may use the table or graph produced by the equation $y = 40(0.75)^x$ to find their response.

Unit 6

Lesson 2 Quiz

Form B

1. The equation of the graph below is of the form $y = a(b)^x$. Will b be less than 1 or greater than 1? Explain your answer.

   Greater ____   *Less* ____
   Explanation:

   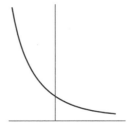

2. Suppose a ball dropped on a hard surface rebounds to half of its drop height. The ball is dropped from 10 feet.

   a. How high will the ball rebound on the first bounce? On the second bounce? Show or explain your work.

      First bounce: _____   *Second bounce:* _____
      Explanation:

   b. Write a *NOW-NEXT* equation that shows how to calculate the rebound height for any bounce from the height of the previous bounce.

      NEXT = _____

   c. Write a rule beginning "$y = \ldots$" that estimates the rebound after any number of bounces.

      $y =$ _____

Lesson 2 Quiz

d. Use the equations from Parts b or c to complete a table showing expected heights after the first five bounces.

Bounce Number	0	1	2	3	4	5
Height (ft)	10					

e. Make a plot of the data from Part d, and then a continuous graph of your "y = ..." rule. Use your calculator (or computer software), then copy the plot and graph below.

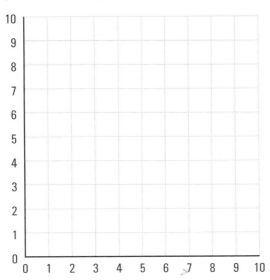

f. On which bounce does the ball first rebound to less than an inch? Explain or show your work.

Bounce number: _____

Explanation:

Suggested Solutions

1. The graph decreases as x increases. A base less than 1 raised to increasing powers, decreases, so the base b must be less than 1.

2. **a.** On the first bounce the ball will rebound 5 feet. On the second bounce the ball will rebound 2.5 feet. On the first bounce, the rebound height is half of the drop height, 10 feet. On the second bounce, the rebound height is half of the drop height, which is now 5 feet, the rebound height for the first bounce.

   b. $NEXT = 0.5 \times NOW$, starting with 10

   c. $y = 10\left(\frac{1}{2}\right)^x$

   d. Heights are rounded to three decimal places.

Bounce Number	0	1	2	3	4	5
Height (ft)	10	5	2.5	1.25	0.625	0.313

   e.

   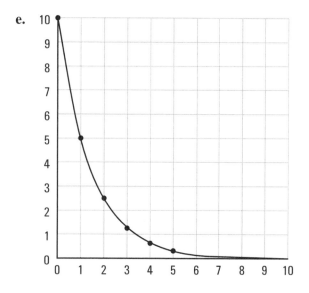

   f. One inch is $\frac{1}{12}$ or 0.0833 ft. The first rebound height that is less than 0.0833 feet occurs on the seventh bounce. Students may extend the table from Part d using repeated multiplication by 0.5, using a guess-and-check method, or using a technology-generated table or graph to find their response.

Unit 6

Lesson 3 Quiz

1. A school fund drive earned $7,000, which was invested in an account that earns interest at a rate of 9% per year.

   a. Complete the table below by entering the amount of money in the account after each year for 5 years.

Time (years)	0	1	2	3	4	5
Amount (dollars)	7,000					

   b. Write a *NOW-NEXT* equation that can be used to calculate the amount in the account at the end of any year, given the amount at the end of the previous year. Explain how your equation fits this situation.

   NEXT = _____

   Explanation:

   c. Write a rule beginning "*y* = …" that can be used to calculate the amount in the account at the end of any number of years. Explain why your rule makes sense.

   y = _____

   Explanation:

   d. How much money will be in the account at the end of 10 years? Show or explain your work.

   Ten-year total: _____

   Work or explanation:

Unit 6

e. Approximately how long will it take for the $7,000 investment to double? Explain how you obtained your response.

Doubling time: _____

Explanation:

f. How much would be in the account at the end of 10 years if the interest rate were 6% instead of 9%? Show or explain your work.

Ten-year total: _____

Work or explanation:

2. Two compound growth situations are represented by Graphs (1) and (2) and also by Tables (A) and (B). For each graph there is a matching table.

   a. Write the number of the graph beside its corresponding table.

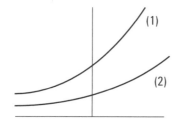

_____ (A)	x	1	2	3	4
	y	2.6	3.38	4.394	5.7122

_____ (B)	x	1	2	3	4
	y	6.5	8.45	10.985	14.281

   b. The equations of the graphs in Part a are of the form $y = a(1.3)^x$. Will a be greater for Graph (1) or for Graph (2)? Explain your answer.

   Greater for (1) ____ *(2)* ____

   Explanation:

   c. Find the value of a so that the model $y = a(1.3)^x$ represents the data in Table (A).

Use after page 460.

Suggested Solutions

1. a.

Time (years)	0	1	2	3	4	5
Amount (dollars)	7,000	7,630	8,316.70	9,065.20	9,881.07	10,770.37

   (**Note:** If students use a table generated by a TI-82 or TI-83, they will have approximate answers.)

   b. $NEXT = NOW \times 0.09 + NOW$ or $NEXT = NOW \times 1.09$

   This means to get the interest for the year, take 9% of the amount you have at the end of the previous year. Then add the interest to the amount at the end of the previous year.

   c. $y = 7000(1.09^x)$

   When $x = 0$, then $y = 7000$. When $x = 1$ (that is, after one year), the amount is $7,000 plus the first year's interest; that is, $7000 + 0.09 \times 7000$ or 7000×1.09. When $x = 2$ (that is, after two years), the amount is the amount after one year, 7000×1.09, times 1.09. Notice that this pattern continues, and it is the same as using the equation $NEXT = NOW \times 1.09$ in Part b.

   d. There will be $7000(1.09^{10}) = \$16,571.55$ in the account after 10 years.

   e. It takes just over 8 years for the $7,000 to double. After 8 years there is $13,947.94.

   f. There would be $12,535.93 in the account after 10 years if the interest rate were 6% instead of 9%. This can be found using $y = 7000(1.06^{10})$.

2. a. Graph (2) corresponds to Table (A); Graph (1) corresponds to Table (B).

   b. The value of a is greater in the equation for Graph (1), since Graph (1) has the larger y-intercept and a corresponds to the value when $x = 0$.

   c. $a = 2$

Unit 6

Lesson 3 Quiz

1. The population of Smallville is 14,000. For planning purposes, the city council assumes Smallville's growth rate is 3% per year.

   a. Complete the table below by giving the predicted population after each of the next 5 years.

Time (years)	0	1	2	3	4	5
Amount (dollars)	14,000					

   b. Write a *NOW-NEXT* equation that gives the predicted population of Smallville at the end of any year, given the population at the end of the previous year.

   NEXT = _____

   c. Write a rule beginning "*y* = ..." that can be used to calculate the predicted population of Smallville at the end of any number of years. Explain why your rule makes sense.

   y = _____

   Explanation:

   d. Find the predicted population of Smallville at the end of 10 years. Show or explain your work.

   Population in 10 years: _____
   Explanation:

   e. Find approximately how long it would take for the population of Smallville to reach 20,000. Explain how you obtained your response.

   Time needed: _____
   Explanation:

Use after page 460.

f. Find the predicted population of Smallville at the end of 10 years if the growth rate is 5% instead of 3% per year. Show or explain your work.

Predicted population _____

Work or explanation:

2. Two compound growth situations are represented by Graphs (1) and (2) and also by Tables (A) and (B). For each graph there is a matching table.

a. Write the number of the graph beside its corresponding table.

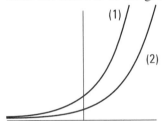

_____ (A)

x	1	2	3	4
y	3.4	5.78	9.826	16.704

_____ (B)

x	1	2	3	4
y	1.36	2.312	3.93	6.6817

b. The equations of the graphs in Part a are of the form $y = a(1.7)^x$. Will a be greater for Graph (1) or for Graph (2)? Explain your answer.

Greater for (1) _____ *(2)* _____

Explanation:

c. Find the value of a so that the model $y = a(1.7)^x$ represents the data in Table (A).

Unit 6

Suggested Solutions

1. **a.**

Time in Years	0	1	2	3	4	5
Population	14,000	14,420	14,853	15,298	15,757	16,230

b. $NEXT = NOW \times 1.03$ or $NEXT = (NOW \times 0.03) + NOW$

c. $y = 14000(1.03^x)$

When $x = 0$, then $y = 14,000$. When $x = 1$ (that is, after one year), the population is 14,000 plus the first year's increase; that is, $14000 + 0.03 \times 14000$ or 14000×1.03. When $x = 2$ (that is, after two years) the new population is the population after one year, $14,000 \times 1.03$, times 1.03. Notice that this pattern continues, and it is the same as using the equation $NEXT = NOW \times 1.03$ in Part b.

d. $14,000(1.03^{10}) \approx 18,815$; the population after 10 years will be approximately 18,815.

e. It takes between 12 and 13 years for the predicted population to reach 20,000.

f. At a 5% increase, the predicted population in 10 years would be $14,000(1.05^{10})$ or approximately 22,805.

2. **a.** Graph (1) corresponds to Table (A); Graph (2) corresponds to Table (B).

b. Because a corresponds to the y-intercept and Graph (1) has the greater y-intercept, a will be greater for Graph (1).

c. $a = 2$

Unit 6

Lesson 4 Quiz

1. The following data were collected by running an experiment in which 20 dice were tossed. All of the dice that showed 2s and 3s were removed, and the remaining dice were tossed. Again, all of the dice showing 2s and 3s were removed, and so on.

Toss Number	0	1	2	3	4	5	6	7	8
Number of Dice Remaining	20	14	8	6	4	2	1	1	1

a. Make a scatterplot of these data.

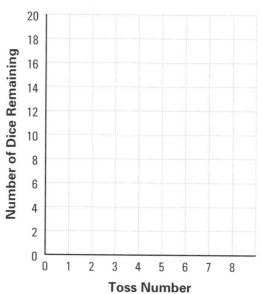

b. What pattern makes it reasonable to think that this is an exponential relation of the form $y = a(b^x)$?

c. Use your calculator or computer software to find an algebraic model that fits the pattern in the data. Explain your steps.

Model: _____

Explanation:

Unit 6

Lesson 4 Quiz

d. In the equation $y = a(b^x)$ for the exponential model, what do the values of a and b tell about the pattern of change?

Meaning of a: *Meaning of b:*

e. Suppose the experiment is changed so that 15 dice were tossed and all of the dice showing 6s were removed. The remaining dice were tossed, again all of the dice showing 6s were removed, and so on. Compare the pattern of (*toss number*, *dice left*) data you would expect from this experiment with the pattern of (*toss number*, *dice left*) pattern observed in the experiment from Parts a–b.

f. What equation would you expect to be a good model for the data in Part e? Explain.

Equation: _____

Explanation:

Suggested Solutions

1. a.

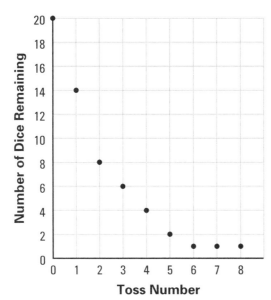

Number of Dice Remaining (y-axis, 0 to 20)
Toss Number (x-axis, 0 to 8)

b. As the toss number increases, the number of dice remaining is about 60% or 70% of the number remaining on the previous toss, suggesting $NEXT \approx 0.7 \times NOW$, an exponential relation.

c. Using a TI-82 or TI-83, enter the data into Lists 1 and 2 and use the exponential regression choice under the STAT, CALC menu. The result is approximately $y = 19.4(0.66)^x$.

d. The starting value or the value of y when $x = 0$ is a. The value of b determines whether the graph of the equation will be increasing (if $b > 1$) or decreasing (if $0 < b < 1$). In this case $0 < b < 1$, so the pattern of change is decreasing at a decreasing rate. For each 1 unit increase in x, the value of y is decreased by $(1 - b)\%$.

e. The starting y value is 15 (because initially there are 15 dice) instead of 20, and the graph will decrease more gradually than in the previous experiment. The decrease is more gradual because you would expect to remove about half as many dice with each toss as was the case in the previous experiment.

f. $y = 15(0.833)^x$

The y-intercept is 15. The value of b is the ratio of dice you would expect to remain after each toss. Since the probability of 6 on any die is $\frac{1}{6}$, you would expect the fraction of dice remaining on each toss to be $\left(1 - \frac{1}{6}\right)$ or approximately 0.833.

Unit 6

Lesson 4 Quiz

1. The following data were collected by running an experiment in which 30 dice were tossed. All of the dice that showed 5s and 6s were removed, and the remaining dice were tossed. Again, all of the dice showing 5s and 6s were removed, and so on.

Toss Number	0	1	2	3	4	5	6	7	8
Number of Dice Remaining	30	20	15	11	8	6	4	3	2

a. Make a scatterplot of these data.

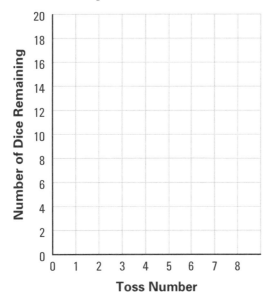

b. What pattern makes it reasonable to think that this is an exponential relation of the form $y = a(b^x)$?

c. Use your calculator or computer software to find an algebraic model that fits the pattern in the data. Explain your steps.

Model: _____

Explanation:

Lesson 4 Quiz

d. In the equation $y = a(b^x)$ for the exponential model, what do the values of a and b tell about the pattern of change?

Meaning of a: *Meaning of b:*

e. Suppose the experiment is changed so that 20 dice were tossed. All of the dice showing 1s were removed and the remaining dice were tossed. Again, all of the dice showing 1s were removed, and so on. Compare the pattern of (*toss number, dice left*) data you would expect from this experiment with the pattern of (*toss number, dice left*) observed in the experiment in Parts a–b.

Unit 6

f. What equation would you expect to be a good model for the data in Part e? Explain.

Equation: _____

Explanation:

Suggested Solutions

1. **a.**

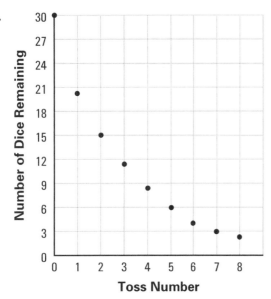

Number of Dice Remaining vs Toss Number

   b. As the toss number increases, the number of dice remaining is about 70% of the number remaining on the previous toss, suggesting *NEXT* ≈ 0.7 × *NOW*, an exponential relation.

   c. Using a TI-82 or TI-83, enter the data into Lists 1 and 2 and use the exponential regression choice under the STAT, CALC menu. The result is approximately $y = 29.3(0.72)^x$.

   d. The starting value or the value of *y* when $x = 0$ is *a*. The value of *b* determines whether the graph of the equation will be increasing (if $b > 1$) or decreasing (if $0 < b < 1$). In this case $0 < b < 1$, so the pattern of change is decreasing at a decreasing rate. For each unit increase in *x*, the *y* value is decreased by $(1 - b)$.

   e. The initial *y* value is 20, and the graph will decrease more gradually than in the previous experiment. The decrease is more gradual because you would expect to remove about half as many dice with each toss as was the case in the previous experiment.

   f. $y = 20(0.833)^x$

   The starting value is 20. The value of *b* is the ratio of dice you would expect to remain after each toss. Since the probability of 1 on any die is $\frac{1}{6}$, you would expect the fraction of dice remaining on each toss to be $(1 - \frac{1}{6})$ or approximately 0.833.

In-Class Exam

1. In a game of Backgammon, the players control how many points a particular game is worth. The minimum score for a winning game is 1 point, and the maximum is 32. At any time in the game, a player may double the current worth.

   a. Make a table showing the point scores for up to 3 changes.

Number of Changes	0	1	2	3	4
Point Score					

   b. Explain how the scores in Part a can be found in at least two different ways using your graphing calculator or computer software.

   First way:

   Second way:

   c. What *NOW-NEXT* equation will help predict the point score for each change?

   NEXT = _____

   d. Using your calculator or computer, find the number of changes that can be made before a player would not be able to double the point score again. Explain.

   Number of changes: _____

   Explanation:

In-Class Exam

2. When she was born, Tabatha's rich aunt put $10,000 in a bank account in Tabatha's name to be saved for her college education. The account earns 6% annual interest.

   a. Make a table showing the value of that account each year for 18 years. Round your answer to the nearest dollar.

Year	Balance ($)	Year	Balance ($)
0	10,000	10	
1		11	
2		12	
3		13	
4		14	
5		15	
6		16	
7		17	
8		18	
9			

   b. Graph the data from your table in Part a.

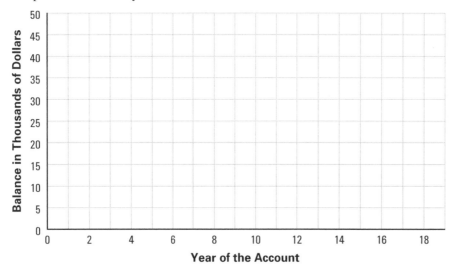

   c. Write a *NOW-NEXT* equation that could be used to calculate the value of the account for any number of years.

   NEXT = _____

Use after page 481.

d. Write an equation beginning "$y = ...$" that could be used to calculate the value of the account for any number of years.

$y = $ _____

e. Find the value of Tabatha's account after 18 years if the interest rate were 10% and the initial deposit were $10,000. Explain how you obtained your result.

Value after 18 years: _____

Explanation:

3. The following table gives the number of AIDS cases reported in the Los Angeles area for the years 1983 through 1988.

Years Since 1983	0	1	2	3	4	5
Number of AIDS Cases Reported	270	466	684	1,441	1,885	1,898

a. Use your calculator or computer software to produce a scatterplot, an equation for a linear model, and an equation for an exponential model.

Linear model: _____

Exponential model: _____

b. Describe the similarities and the differences between the tables and graphs produced by these equations.

Similarities: *Differences:*

c. Which model, linear or exponential, do you think would be a better predictor of the number of AIDS cases in Los Angeles at the end of the 1990s and beyond? Explain why you think so.

Linear _____   *Exponential* _____

Explanation:

Unit 6

Suggested Solutions

1. a.

Number of Changes	0	1	2	3
Point Score	1	2	4	8

   b. One way is to enter 1 * 2 and press the ENTER key for the first change. Then press ⊠ 2 ENTER for the second change and press ENTER again for change 3. A second way to find the score after n changes is to press 2 ∧ n ENTER. There are other ways, of course.

   c. $NEXT = 2 \times NOW$

   d. On the fifth change, the maximum score allowed (32) is reached.

2. a.

Year	Balance ($)	Year	Balance ($)
0	10,000	10	17,908
1	10,600	11	18,983
2	11,236	12	20,122
3	11,910	13	21,329
4	12,625	14	22,609
5	13,382	15	23,966
6	14,185	16	25,404
7	16,036	17	26,928
8	15,938	18	28,543
9	16,895		

Suggested Solutions (*continued*)

b.

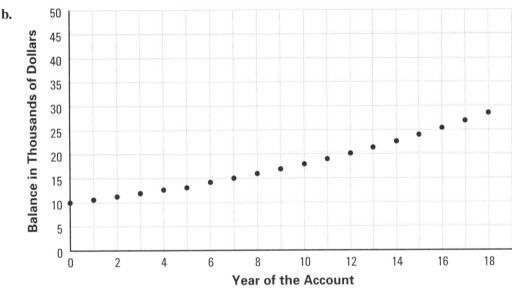

c. $NEXT = 1.06 \times NOW$

d. $y = 10,000(1.06)^x$

e. If the interest rate were 10%, the balance after 10 years would be $55,599.

3. a. Approximate linear regression equation: $y = 376x + 168$
   Approximate exponential equation: $y = 306(1.52)^x$

b. The tables and the graphs for both models show that the number of AIDS cases reported in Los Angeles has been increasing since 1983. The linear model shows a constant increase of about 376 cases per year. But the exponential model (both table and graph) shows that the number of new AIDS cases reported each year in L.A. is increasing at an increasing rate. The graph of the linear model is a line and the graph of the exponential model is a curve.

c. Students may choose either model. Be sure they support their choice. Those choosing the linear model may be focusing on the fact that the number of AIDS cases seems to be leveling off, not growing at an increasing rate. Students choosing the exponential model will probably be focusing on the fact that at least until 1988 the number of cases was growing at an increasing rate.

Unit 6

In-Class Exam

1. In a movie, an absent-minded professor invented a substance called flubber. When a ball made of flubber was dropped from a particular height, it would bounce twice as high as the distance from which it was dropped. For example, a ball dropped from 1 foot would bounce 2 feet on the first bounce, 4 feet on the second bounce, and so on. Flubber, of course, got the professor in one comical situation after another, including a basketball game in which the home team wore shoes with flubber soles which allowed them to jump over the rafters of the gymnasium.

   a. Make a table showing the height that a flubber ball dropped from 1 foot would bounce in each of the first 10 bounces.

Bounce Number	1	2	3	4	5	6	7	8	9	10
Height (feet)										

   b. Suppose when basketball players with flubber-soled shoes jumped several times, the height of each jump followed the same pattern as in the above table. If the players jumped one foot high on their first jump, on what jump would their feet go over a rafter that is 100 feet above the floor? Explain your response.

   Jump number: _____

   Explanation:

   c. Explain how the answers to Parts a and b can be found in at least two different ways using your graphing calculator or computer software.

   First way:

   Second way:

Unit 6

In-Class Exam

2. A plastic material used for sun visors allows light to pass through, but reduces the light's intensity. A one-millimeter thick sheet of this plastic reduces the intensity of light by 10%. An additional millimeter reduces the resulting light by 10%, and so on.

a. Complete the following table showing the pattern of the percentage of light passing through sheets of this plastic.

Thickness (mm)	1	2	3	4	5	6	7	8	9	10
Percent of Light Passing	90									

b. Graph the data in your table in Part a.

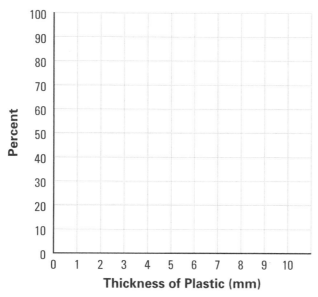

c. For what thickness of plastic sheet will the light passing through first be less than 50% of its actual intensity?

Thickness: _____

Unit 6

d. Write an equation beginning "*y* = … " that can be used to calculate the percentage of the light that passes through a plastic sheet with any thickness (measured in millimeters).

y = _____

3. In 1990, the population of the United States was about 249 million people. The annual rate of growth in the population is about 1%.

a. Make a table showing the predicted population, to the nearest million, of the U.S. for the six years from 1991 to 1996.

Years Since 1990	1	2	3	4	5	6
Predicted Population						

b. Write a *NOW-NEXT* equation that could be used to calculate U.S. population estimates for a year based on the previous year's population.

NEXT = _____

c. Write an equation beginning "*y* = …" that could be used to calculate U.S. population estimates any number of years after 1990.

y = _____

d. Use the equation in Part b or c to estimate the population of the U.S. in 2020.

Population in 2020: _____

e. The number in Part d is a prediction based on growth patterns up to 1994. What factors might cause the U.S. population in 2020 to be different from this prediction?

Unit 6

Suggested Solutions

1. **a.**

Bounce Number	1	2	3	4	5	6	7	8	9	10
Height (feet)	2	4	8	16	32	64	128	256	512	1,024

b. On jump 7, the players would jump 128 feet above the ground and well above the rafters, as the table in Part a shows.

c. One way is to enter 2 $\times$ 2 and press $\boxed{\text{ENTER}}$ for jump 2. Press $\boxed{\times}$ 2 $\boxed{\text{ENTER}}$ for jump 3 and then press $\boxed{\text{ENTER}}$ once for each jump 4, 5, and 6. A second way to find jump n is to press 2 $\boxed{\wedge}$ n $\boxed{\text{ENTER}}$. A third way is to enter $y = (2)^x$ in the functions list and check the table or graph for values.

2. **a.**

Thickness (mm)	1	2	3	4	5	6	7	8	9	10
Percent of Light Passing	90	81	73	66	59	53	48	43	39	35

b.

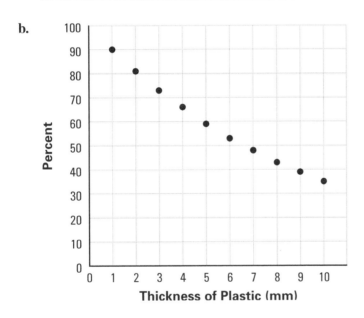

c. A 7-mm-thick sheet will allow only 48% of the light through, as the table in Part a shows.

d. $y = 100(0.9)^x$

Unit 6

Suggested Solutions (*continued*)

3. **a.**

Years Since 1990	1	2	3	4	5	6
Predicted Population	251	254	257	259	262	264

b. $NEXT = NOW + (0.01) \times NOW$ or $NEXT = 1.01 \times NOW$

c. $y = 249(1.01)^x$

d. The year 2020 is 30 years after 1990, so the population estimate is $249(1.01)^{30}$ or approximately 336 million.

e. People decide how many children to have, so there could be a slower increase if campaigns to decrease the birth rate were successful. On the other hand, such campaigns may fail, thereby making the prediction too low. Other factors like war, epidemics of fatal diseases, and natural disasters (earthquakes, floods, and so forth) tend to keep the population down. There are many other possible social and economic factors that could be mentioned.

Take-Home Assessment

1. Write answers to the Checkpoint at the end of this unit. Then write a one-hour exam that tests the ability to understand and apply all the main ideas in the Checkpoint. Include a summary page with your exam that indicates which exam problems, or parts of problems, correspond to each of the five parts of the Checkpoint.

2. In Investigation 2 (pp. 443–444), you learned about a famous fractal pattern called a Sierpinski carpet. There is a three-dimensional version of this fractal called a *Sierpinski cube*. The Sierpinski cube is formed using the three-dimensional version of the same stages that are illustrated in Investigation 2 (page 443). Start with a cube made from straws and pipe cleaners and construct the first stage of a Sierpinski cube. Consider the volume of the original cube to be one cubic unit.

   a. How much of the original cube remains after the first step or "cutout"?

   Imagine continuing this pattern of removing parts of the cube several more times, and answer these questions.

   b. What fraction of the cube left by the first cutout remains after the second cutout? How much of the original one cubic unit of volume remains after the second cutout?

   c. What fraction of the cube left by the second cutout remains after the third cutout? How much of the original one cubic unit of volume remains after the third cutout?

   d. How much of the original one cubic unit of volume remains after the fourth cutout? After the fifth cutout?

   e. What equation shows the relation between volume remaining at any stage *NOW* and the *NEXT* stage?

   f. What volumes would you predict for the "cube" left after cutouts 10? 20? 30?

   g. What equation would allow you to calculate the volume *y* of the remaining part of the cube after any cutout stage *x* without going through all the stages from 1 to *x*?

Unit 6

Take-Home Assessment

3. The following table gives the population (in millions) of three states and the United States for each census from 1900 through 1990.

State	1900	1910	1920	1930	1940	1950	1960	1970	1980	1990
Arizona	0.12	0.20	0.33	0.44	0.50	0.75	1.30	1.78	2.71	3.67
Michigan	2.42	2.81	3.67	4.84	5.26	6.37	7.82	8.89	9.26	9.30
Vermont	0.28	0.36	0.35	0.36	0.36	0.38	0.39	0.44	0.51	0.56
U.S.	76.2	92.2	106.0	123.2	132.2	151.3	179.3	203.3	226.5	248.7

a. Plot these data and examine the patterns. Does the U.S. population over time appear to follow a linear or an exponential pattern?

b. For which states is the pattern of population change approximately linear? Approximately exponential?

c. Use your calculator or computer software to find a linear or exponential model, as appropriate, for the population growth of each state and of the entire country. (Use $x = 0$ for 1900, $x = 1$ for 1910, and so forth.)

d. Explain what the patterns and models mean about the population in each state. Give some plausible reasons for the state-by-state differences.

Unit 6

Each one of these take-home assessments should be done over one to three days.

1. Exams will vary, but encourage students to write thoughtful questions that cover the main ideas in the closing Checkpoint. It would also be interesting for other students to work on and critique the exams of their classmates.

2. Note: Building the cube is difficult and time-consuming. Students need to make a large cube and a small one, with sides one-third those of the large cube. They also will need to connect (with straws) the vertices of the large cube to those of the small cube in order to suspend the small cube at the center of the large one.

   a. $\frac{26}{27}$ of the volume still remains. The center cube that is removed is one of 27 equal parts.

   b. $\frac{26}{27}$ of the volume after cutout 1 is still left; $\frac{26}{27} \cdot \frac{26}{27}$ (that is, $\frac{676}{729}$ or approximately 0.927) of the original cube remains.

   c. Again, $\frac{26}{27}$ of the volume after cutout 2 is still left; that is about 0.893 of the original cube.

   d. Raise $\frac{26}{27}$ to the fourth and fifth powers, getting about 0.860 and 0.828, respectively.

   e. $NEXT = NOW \times \frac{26}{27}$

   f. After the cutout, the volume of the cube will be approximately 0.686. After the 20th cutout, the volume of the cube will be approximately 0.470. After the 30th cutout, the volume of the cube will be approximately 0.322.

   g. $y = \left(\frac{26}{27}\right)^x$

3. a.

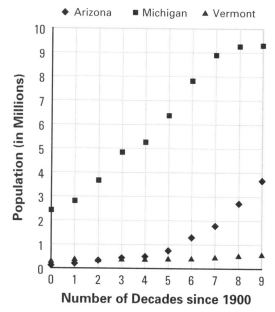

◆ Arizona   ■ Michigan   ▲ Vermont

Population (in Millions) vs. Number of Decades since 1900

Unit 6

Unit 6

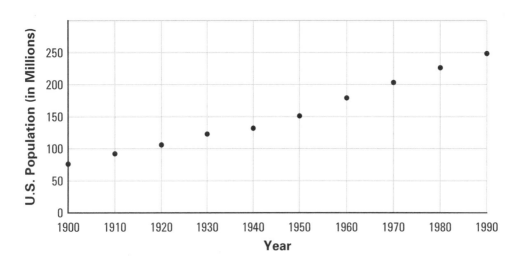

The pattern of the U.S. population over these years appears to be approximately linear, although it increases somewhat more rapidly in later years as an exponential model does.

b. The pattern for Vermont appears to be approximately linear, and the pattern for Arizona appears to be exponential. Michigan's population grew fairly rapidly and approximately linearly from 1900 to 1970, but then after that it remained more or less constant.

c. Arizona: One exponential model is $y = 0.13(1.45)^x$.
Michigan is neither linear nor exponential.
Vermont: One linear model is $y = 0.025x + 0.29$.
United States: One linear model is $y = 19.2x + 67.5$.
   One exponential model is $y = 80.1(1.14)^x$.

d. From 1900 to 1990, Arizona's population has approximately followed the exponential model given in Part c. This means that Arizona's population increased at a more rapid rate (as powers of 1.45) from one census to the next. Michigan's pattern of population growth is described in Part b. Vermont's population is approximated by the linear model given in Part c. This means Vermont's population grew from 0.28 to 0.56 million at an approximately constant rate of 0.025 million from one census to the next. The population of the United States grew at an approximately constant rate of 19.2 million from one census to the next, although for later data the rate of increase was somewhat greater and for earlier data somewhat less than 19.2. The exponential model for the United States suggests that the rate increased by a factor of approximately 1.14.

Project

Comparing Real Investment Plans

Purpose

In this unit, you learned that money invested in an interest bearing account grows exponentially. In this project, you will gather data concerning the exact terms of several investment plans available in your community. Using these data, you will compare the plans and describe the strengths and weaknesses of each.

Directions

1. Go to one or more banks or a Savings & Loan Office in your community. Ask for written descriptions of at least three investment plans, such as passbook savings, certificates of deposit of differing lengths, and savings bonds.

2. If possible, talk with a bank officer or other informed person about this project. Ask this person to verify your understanding of the terms of the investment plan and exactly how and when the interest is earned. In addition, inquire concerning the purposes and strengths of each plan. For example, is the money available upon request and with no penalty at any time, or is there a penalty for early withdrawal?

3. Using the terms of each investment plan, compute the value of an investment of $1,000 after 1, 5, and 10 years with each plan. Be sure to deduct any penalties for early withdrawal.

4. Write a report in which you describe the terms of the investment plans that you examined. Report the results of your computations in Part 3 above. Based on these results and the printed and oral information from the bank, describe the strengths and weaknesses of each investment plan. The strengths and weaknesses will depend to some extent on the purposes of the investment. For example, one plan may be better if you are saving for a vacation or to buy a car, another may be better if you are saving for college in three years, and still another may be better if you are getting an early start on a retirement plan that you will use in thirty or forty years.

Unit 6

Project

Comparing Real Investment Plans

This project can best be done by a pair or small group of students, since students may need support from one another when they interview a bank officer. The purpose is for students to anchor what they learned about interest in this unit to real investment plans in their own communities. Important practical issues such as the liquidity of the investment, its term, and penalties for early withdrawal should arise during this project. Furthermore, the importance of each of these issues depends on the purposes of the investment. This project should be especially useful to students in adult life, and it also will help them better appreciate and remember the mathematics of interest.

Suggested Timeline

Allow groups of students a day or two to plan their approach to this project and get approval from you. Students should have several days to a week to gather and analyze their data. It would be good to have them submit an outline before they begin to write the report so you can give them early feedback. Allow another few days for them to submit the first draft of their report. Give them feedback, and then allow a week after that for the final report. You might allow some class time for different groups who are working on this project to compare their approaches and findings to that point.

Report Format

Guidelines for your students might be similar to the following.

Your report should demonstrate that you understand how an investment will grow in each of the investment plans that you choose to analyze. You will need to include:

- descriptions of each plan;
- results of the computations for each plan and;
- analysis of the strengths and weaknesses of each plan.

Remember that the purposes of the investment may influence which plan is the best. Be sure to take this into consideration when you are analyzing the different plans. Also, you should always check your calculations and proofread your report before you turn it in.

Suggested Evaluation Criteria

1. The format of the report follows directions.	20%
2. Appropriateness of choice and descriptions of investment institutions and plans	20%
3. Accuracy of and quality of reporting income computations	20%
4. Choice and accuracy of investment purposes that are discussed	20%
5. Strengths and weaknesses are accurately based on investment purposes.	20%

Project

Population Trends in Your School

Purpose

In this unit and previous ones, you have explored trends in population. For this project you will gather data concerning such trends in your own school district. Your description and analysis of the data may provide some useful information for your local school board.

Directions

1. Work through your teacher and the school administration to get the current enrollment figures for each grade in your district, K through 12. Discuss this project with an administrator or counselor in your school to see if there is particular related information in which they are interested, such as numbers in particular geographic areas within the district or numbers of boys compared to girls. Questions that may be of interest are the need for more buildings, more or fewer teachers, planning future bus routes, or adjusting boundaries for particular schools in the district.

2. Plot the data by year and according to any other characteristics, like the ones named above, that are of interest to you or your school administration. Examine the patterns in the plots, noting whether there is decline or growth over time and what mathematical model fits the pattern in the data.

3. Write a report describing your procedures and findings, including tables and plots of your data and your interpretation of them. For each characteristic you have chosen, describe what information you believe your data have to offer, and how and why that information may be limited. Make specific recommendations concerning future plans in your district, if any seem to be warranted. These plans may include gathering more data or pursuing an action like a building project, changing school boundaries, or changing bus routes.

4. Present your report to your teacher and any parents, school administrators, or school board members who may be interested in your findings. An oral report at a meeting or an article in the local newspaper may even be appropriate.

Unit 6

Population Trends in Your School

This project probably could be done best by a small group of students, as it has several parts and it is likely to involve some interesting discussions and interpretation of the data. You may want to talk to your principal or another administrator about this project before students begin to contact them. This will give the administrator a chance to think about real district issues that might be informed by the project and to decide whether it would be acceptable for students to get involved in the issue. Even if there is no pressing current issue, the project will still be a good exercise for students in gathering, analyzing, and presenting data that are of local interest.

Suggested Timeline

As suggested above, check with administrators yourself to get their input concerning possible directions for this project. When you assign the project, inform the students of what you learned from the administrators and define local guidelines for when and how to contact the administrators and what issue to address. Allow groups of students a day or two to plan their approach to the project. Students should have several days to a week to gather, plot, and analyze their data. Allow another few days for them to submit the first draft of their report. Give them feedback, and then allow a week after that for the final report. Be sure to have them report the results to any interest groups such as administrators, other teachers, or parents.

Report Format

Guidelines for your students might be similar to the following.

Your report should explain the purpose of the project and the procedures that you used to gather, plot, and analyze the data. It should include tables and plots that are relevant to your interpretation of the data. You need to discuss both the strengths and the limitations of your interpretation, as well as recommendations for future actions. If appropriate, you also will need to prepare and present an oral report to administrators or local interest groups.

Suggested Evaluation Criteria

1. The format of the report follows directions.   20%
2. The plots and tables of data are accurate and clearly presented.   20%
3. Appropriate interpretation of the data for the project's purpose   20%
4. Recommendations are clearly presented and supported by the data.   20%
5. Clear and interesting oral report   20%

Lesson 1 Quiz

1. Suppose a population control plan for the country of Transylvania allows parents to have at most four children each, and they must stop having children when they get two girls. Explain how to use a coin to simulate the experiment of having children until you have either two girls or four children.

2. Romula was exposed to a cold virus, and now he has a 50% chance of developing a cold on each of the next 7 days. A simulation was run in which a fair coin was tossed.

   Heads = develops a cold   **T**ails = does not develop a cold

   Each coin toss represents one day. So, for example, TTH means that Romula developed a cold on the third day, and TTTTTTT means no cold in 7 days.

   a. Complete the frequency table for the given simulation results.

Develops a Cold on Day Number	Frequency
1	
2	
3	
4	
5	
6	
7	

TTH	TTH
TH	TH
TH	TTTH
TH	H
TTTTTH	H
TTTH	TTTTTTH
TTTH	TTTTH

Lesson 1 Quiz

b. Construct a histogram for the frequency table in Part a.

c. Using the frequency table or histogram, estimate the average number of days that it took Romula to develop a cold.

Estimate: _____

d. Using the frequency table or histogram, estimate the percent of times that Romula will develop a cold before the third day.

Estimate: _____

Suggested Solutions

1. Let heads represent having a boy and tails represent having a girl. Since the parents can have at most four children, the coin can be tossed no more than four times for each simulation trial. Furthermore, since the parents must stop having children when they get two girls, a trial ends if and when tails is flipped twice.

2. **a.**

Develops a Cold on Day Number	Frequency
1	2
2	4
3	2
4	3
5	1
6	1
7	1

b.

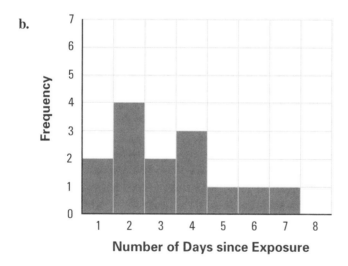

Number of Days since Exposure

c. The estimate of the average number of days to develop a cold is 3.286, found by computing

$$\frac{(1 \cdot 2) + (2 \cdot 4) + (3 \cdot 2) + (4 \cdot 3) + (5 \cdot 1) + (6 \cdot 1) + (7 \cdot 1)}{14}$$

Students may say about 3 days, since this item asks for an estimate.

d. Romula developed a cold before the third day in 6 of 14 trials, so the best estimate is 43%.

Unit 7

Lesson 1 Quiz

1. Ms. Jefferson is writing a 15-item true-false test for her Algebra class. For each of items 1 through 15, she decides randomly whether to write a true statement or a false statement. Explain how to use a coin to simulate the correct answers on Ms. Jefferson's test.

2. Andrea and Shawna, finalists in a checkers tournament, are to play five games. Each has a 50% chance of winning any game. A simulation was run in which a balanced coin was tossed where:

   H = Andrea wins   **T** = Shawna wins

   a. Complete the frequency table for the given simulation results.

Number of Wins for Andrea	Frequency
0	
1	
2	
3	
4	
5	

HTHHT	TTTTT
HTTHT	HTTTH
THHTH	THHHT
TTHTH	THHHT
HHTTH	HHTHT
HTTTT	HTTTH
THTTH	HTHTT
TTHTT	HHTHT
THTTT	HTTHH
TTTTH	HHTHH

Lesson 1 Quiz

b. Construct a histogram from the frequency table in Part a.

c. Using the histogram or frequency table, estimate the average number of wins for Andrea in a five-game set.

Estimate: _____

d. Estimate the average number of wins for Shawna in a five-game set. Explain how you arrived at your estimate.

Estimate: _____

Explanation:

Suggested Solutions

1. Let heads represent true and tails represent false. Since Ms. Jefferson decides randomly if each item is true or false, a coin should be tossed for each of the 15 items.

2. a.

Number of Wins for Andrea	Frequency
0	1
1	4
2	6
3	8
4	1
5	0

b.

c. The average number of wins for Andrea is 2.2.

$$\frac{(0 \cdot 1) + (1 \cdot 4) + (2 \cdot 6) + (3 \cdot 8) + (4 \cdot 1) + (5 \cdot 0)}{20} = 2.2$$

d. In this simulation Shawna wins the games that Andrea loses, so Shawna's average number of wins is $5 - 2.2 = 2.8$. In the long run, both will average about 2.5 wins in 5 games.

Alternatively, students may choose to create a frequency table for the number of times Shawna wins, and then find her average number of wins.

Use after page 497.

Lesson 2 Quiz

You will need a table of random digits or your calculator.

1. Teri loves licorice jellybeans. Just for fun, Elaine gives her a bag (that she cannot see through) containing one each of orange, cherry, lemon, lime, and licorice jellybeans.

    a. Without looking, Teri reaches into the bag and takes out one jellybean. What is the probability that she takes out the licorice jellybean?

    Probability: _____

    b. If Teri does not get the licorice jellybean, she gives the jellybean to Elaine. Then, without looking, she reaches into the bag for another jellybean. If that one is not licorice, she gives it to Elaine and reaches in for a third jellybean. Does the chance that Teri will take out the licorice jellybean increase, decrease, or remain the same for each draw? Explain.

    Increase _____   *Decrease* _____   *Remain same* _____

    Explanation:

    c. Design a simulation model that uses a table of random digits or your calculator to estimate the probability that Teri has to take out all five jellybeans before she gets the licorice one.

Unit 7

Lesson 2 Quiz

d. Conduct your simulation 10 times. Add your results to the frequency table below so that there is a total of 1,000 trials. Record the total results in the "Frequency (After)" column.

Number of Jellybeans Teri Needs to Take Out Licorice	Frequency (Before)	Frequency (After)
1	203	
2	196	
3	202	
4	188	
5	201	
Total	990	1,000

e. Using the completed table, estimate the probability that Teri will have to take out all five jellybeans before she gets the licorice one. Explain how you obtained your result.

Probability: _____

Explanation:

Suggested Solutions

1. **a.** One-fifth or 0.2

    b. The chance increases from 1 of 5 (0.2), to 1 of 4 (0.25), to 1 of 3 (0.33), and so on. The number of jellybeans left in the bag after each draw is decreasing, while the number of licorice jellybeans is staying the same. So Teri's chance of drawing the licorice jellybean increases on each draw.

    c. Use a table of random digits or the calculator command "int 5 rand + 1". One way is to assign 1 through 5 to each of the kinds of jellybeans, with 5 representing licorice. Ignore the other digits. When a digit comes up, say 2, it must be skipped after that. When 5 comes up, the trial ends. Start over after each trial.

    d. Results will depend on the outcomes of the 10 trials.

    e. Evaluate the frequency of

    $$\frac{\text{needing to grab five jellybeans}}{1000}$$

    Individual student results should be approximately 0.2.

Lesson 2 Quiz

You will need a table of random digits or your calculator.

1. Jon did not study for a 50-item multiple choice test, and he has no reasonable guesses on any of the questions. He circles a, b, c, d, or e at random. Ms. Perez, his teacher, decided to make "e" the correct answer for every item on the test.

   a. Describe a simulation model for finding the number of the first item on the test that Jon answers correctly.

   b. Perform your simulation five times. The frequency table below has the results of 95 simulations. Add your five results to the frequency table below so that there is a total of 100 trials. Record the total results in the "Frequency (After)" column.

Number of Item	Frequency (Before)	Frequency (After)	Number of Item	Frequency (Before)	Frequency (After)
1	20		10	2	
2	17		11	1	
3	11		12	2	
4	10		13	2	
5	9		14	1	
6	5		15	1	
7	6		16	0	
8	3		17	0	
9	4		18	1	
			Total	95	100

   c. What is the average number of the first item Jon answers correctly?

   Average number: _____

© 1998 Everyday Learning Corporation

Unit 7

Lesson 2 Quiz

d. Based on your simulation, what is your estimate of the probability of Jon getting at least one of the first five questions correct?

Estimate: _____

e. Describe a simulation model for finding the total number of questions Jon answers correctly.

Unit 7

Suggested Solutions

1. **a.** Possible simulations:

   - Using a table of random digits, let a = 0 or 1; b = 2 or 3; c = 4 or 5; d = 6 or 7; and e = 8 or 9. Start at a random spot on the table. Count the numbers until you get an 8 or 9.

   - Use 1–5 for a–e and ignore other digits. Count the number of 1s–4s until you get a 5.

   - Generate random numbers by using "int 5 rand + 1" on a calculator to produce a = 1, b = 2, c = 3, d = 4, e = 5. Then run trials counting the number of times you can press ENTER before you generate a 5.

   b. The answer will depend on results of the student's five trials.

   c. The answer will depend on results of the student's five trials. It is found by multiplying the frequency times the number of items, adding all these and then dividing by 100. Most answers should be near 4.6 (the theoretical average is approximately 5.0).

   d. Responses will vary from 0.67 to 0.72.

   Students should evaluate

   $$\frac{\text{sum of first five rows of "Frequency (After)" column}}{100}$$

   e. Students can use the same random number assignments that they used in Part a. However, the definition of one trial will be different. In this case, one trial will be considering 50 random numbers and counting how many of them correspond with getting the correct answer.

Lesson 3 Quiz

You will need a table of random digits or your calculator.

1. Pat is a basketball player with career 60% free-throw-shooting percentage.

   a. Describe a simulation model to determine the number of free throws Pat can expect to make out of 10 tries.

   b. Conduct five trials of your simulation. Add your results to the frequency table below so there is a total of 400 trials. Record the total results in the "Frequency (After)" column.

Number Made	Frequency (Before)	Frequency (After)	Number Made	Frequency (Before)	Frequency (After)
1	1		6	141	
2	3		7	67	
3	10		8	16	
4	40		9	14	
5	101		10	2	
			Total	395	400

   c. Using this frequency table, what is your estimate of the probability that Pat will make fewer than 5 free throws in 10 tries? Explain how you obtained your response.

   Probability: _____

   Explanation:

Unit 7

2. The histogram below shows the results of 400 repetitions of a simulation. The situation is the same as in Task 1 except that Pat shoots 50 free throws each time.

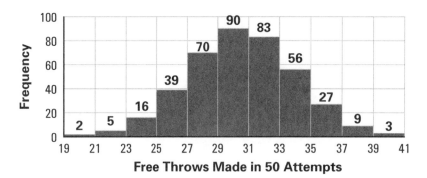

a. Estimate the probability that Pat will make fewer than half of the 50 free throws. Show or explain your work.

Probability: _____

Work or explanation:

b. How does the difference in the probabilities in Task 1 Part c and Task 2 Part a above illustrate the Law of Large Numbers?

c. Estimate the probability that Pat would make fewer than half of 200 free throws. Explain.

Estimate: _____

Explanation:

Suggested Solutions

1. **a.** Using a table of random digits or the calculator command "int 10 rand", let 60% of the digits represent Pat making the free throw (say, 0, 1, 2, 3, 4, 5) and let the rest (6, 7, 8, 9) represent Pat missing the free throw.

   b. The exact result will depend on the outcomes of the students' trials.

   c. The results will depend on the outcomes of the students' trials. The sum of the frequencies for making 1, 2, 3, or 4 free throws should be divided by 400. Students' results should be approximately 0.135.

2. **a.** $\dfrac{2 + 5 + 16}{400} = 0.0575$

   b. According to the Law of Large Numbers, the larger the sample size, the smaller the variance from the value 60%.

   c. Again, the Law of Large Numbers tells us that the probability that Pat will make fewer than half of the 200 free throws would be less than 0.0575, the result for a sample of size 50 free throws. (In fact, the probability will be about 0.01 or very close to 0.)

Unit 7

Lesson 3 Quiz

You will need a table of random digits or your calculator.

1. Suppose Eldorado High School's baseball team has a 70% chance of winning each game it plays against Lansing High School's team.

    a. Describe a simulation model of a series of 5 games between Eldorado and Lansing, in which the first team to win 3 games wins the series.

    b. Conduct 5 trials of your simulation. Add your results to the frequency table below so that there is a total of 100 trials. Record the total results in the "Frequency (After)" column.

Number of Games Needed in the Series	Frequency (Before)	Frequency (After)
3	36	
4	32	
5	27	
Total	95	100

    c. Using this frequency table, what is your estimate of the probability that the teams will play all 5 games? Explain how you obtained your response.

    Probability: _____

    Explanation:

Lesson 3 Quiz

d. Conduct your simulation in Part a 10 times, and record the number of series wins by each team.

Eldorado wins series _____   *Lansing wins series* _____

e. How certain should you be that your results in Part d give a good estimate of the probability that either team will win? Explain.

Very certain _____   *Not very certain* _____

Explanation:

f. Lansing's chances of winning a playoff game against Eldorado are 30%. Are Lansing's chances of winning a best-of-five series more than, less than, or equal to 30%? Explain.

More than 30% _____   *Less than 30%* _____   *Equal to 30%* _____

Explanation:

g. How does the Law of Large Numbers help explain your answers in Parts e and f?

Unit 7

Suggested Solutions

1. **a.** Using a table of random digits or the calculator command "int 10 rand", let 0, 1, 2, 3, 4, 5, or 6 mean Eldorado wins a game, and the other digits mean that Lansing wins. Stop each trial when one team has won 3 games. Then start over for the next trial.

    b. The results will vary depending on the outcomes of the students' trials.

    c. The results will vary depending on the outcome of the students' trials. The probability is computed by dividing the frequency of playing 5 games by 100. Students' results should be between 0.27 and 0.32.

    d. Results will depend on the students' simulation results.

    e. Not very certain. The number of simulations is too small to be confident that the estimate is accurate.

    f. Less than 30%. The longer series gives the better team the advantage. Here, a one-game series is compared to a five-game series.

    g. The Law of Large Numbers says that the experimental probability will get closer to the theoretical probability as the number of trials increases.

Use after page 525.

© 1998 Everyday Learning Corporation

In-Class Exam

You will need a table of random digits or your calculator.

1. At the end of a daily television game show, the contestant who has won the most money is given a chance to win a grand prize. The grand prize is placed randomly behind one of three doors. A substantial cash prize is placed behind a second door, and a "clunker" behind the third. The contestant chooses one of the doors and wins the prize that is behind it.

    a. Explain how you can use a table of random digits to simulate the door a contestant chooses on this game show.

    b. Describe a simulation model that uses your calculator's random number generator to estimate the average number of shows until someone wins a grand prize. (On each show, the winning contestant has three equally likely doors to choose from, and the numbering starts over each time there is a grand prize winner.)

    c. Run the simulation in Part b 10 times. Record the results in the table below, making new rows as needed.

Number of Shows until Grand Prize is Won	Frequency
0	
1	
2	
3	
4	
5	
6	
7	

Unit 7

d. From your 10 simulation runs, compute the average number of shows until someone wins the grand prize.   Explain how you obtained your response.

Average number: _____

Explanation:

2. a. Describe how to use a table of random numbers or your calculator to simulate the sum when two six-sided dice (numbered 1 through 6 on the faces) are tossed.

b. Run the simulation 5 times. Add your results to the frequency table below so that there is a total of 200 trials. Use the "Frequency (After)" column to record the final results.

Number Made	Frequency (Before)	Frequency (After)	Number Made	Frequency (Before)	Frequency (After)
2	4		8	25	
3	11		9	22	
4	13		10	19	
5	20		11	8	
6	27		12	7	
7	39		**Total**	195	200

Use after page 528.

© 1998 Everyday Learning Corporation

In-Class Exam

c. Make a histogram of the data in Part b.

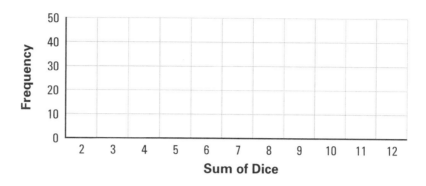

d. Describe the shape of the histogram in Part c. Explain what this shape tells you about the probabilities of various sums occurring when two dice are rolled.

Description of shape:

Probabilities of various sums:

3. A recent survey found that about 80% of Americans believe that communities should have programs to recycle waste material.

a. Assuming this is true, describe how to use a table of random digits or calculator to simulate whether a randomly chosen American believes that communities should have programs to recycle waste material.

Unit 7

In-Class Exam

b. Describe how to use your simulation to estimate how many in a random sample of 30 adults believe that communities should have programs to recycle waste material.

c. Perform 5 trials of your simulation in Part b. Add your results to the frequency table below so that there is a total of 100 trials.

Number Who Want Recycling Programs	Frequency (Before)	Frequency (After)
19	1	
20	3	
21	4	
22	5	
23	12	
24	11	
25	19	
26	15	
27	14	
28	7	
29	4	
30	0	
Total	95	100

d. Using the data in Part c, estimate the probability that more than 25 out of 30 adults who are asked will believe that communities should have programs to recycle waste material? Explain how you obtained your response.

Probability: _____

Explanation:

Suggested Solutions

1. **a.** One way is to let 1, 4, and 7 represent door 1, let 2, 5, and 8 represent door 2, and let 3, 6, and 9 represent door 3. Ignore 0. Then enter the random number table to make the contestant's selection. The contestant wins the prize behind the door that is chosen.

   b. Simulate the game on the calculator by using the command "int 3 rand + 1". Let 1 represent the grand prize, 2 the cash prize, and 3 the "clunker." Run the simulation until the grand prize is won. Record the number of times that were required until it is won. Repeat this process often enough to get an accurate estimate.

   c. The results depend on the outcomes of the student's trials. One simulation of ten trials produced the table below.

Number of Shows Until Grand Prize is Won	Frequency
0	3
1	3
2	0
3	1
4	0
5	1
6	1
7	1

   d. The results depend on the outcomes of the students' trials. The average can be found by multiplying the number of shows by the frequency with which it occurred, adding these products, and dividing by 10. Theoretically, the average is 2.

2. **a.** Using the command "int 6 rand + 1", let 1, 2, 3, 4, 5, and 6 represent the result of tossing a die. Generate two random numbers. Use the first of these numbers for the result on the first die and the second as the result on the second die. Then add the two numbers.

   One way to use the random digits table would be to use only the numbers 1 to 6, ignoring the other numbers. Then add pairs of numbers as you read along the table.

   b. The results will depend on the outcomes of the students' trials.

   c. The results depend on the outcomes of the students' trials.

Unit 7

Suggested Solutions (*continued*)

    d. The histogram will be fairly symmetric and approximately normal. This means that the middle number, 7, is most likely, and the extreme numbers, 2 and 12, are least likely. Pairs of numbers the same distance from 7, like 6 and 8, 5 and 9, and so forth, occur with equal probabilities (although this may not be evident from the students' histograms).

3. a. One way is to let 0 through 7 mean that a person believes that communities should have programs to recycle waste material. Let the other digits mean that person does not believe this. The appropriate calculator command for this simulation would be "int 10 rand".

    b. Repeat the simulation in Part a 30 times and record the number of "believers" in those 30. This would be one trial. Start over and repeat this process often enough to get a good estimate by averaging all results.

    c. The results will depend on the outcomes of the students' trials.

    d. The results depend on the outcomes of the students' trials. The probability can be estimated by adding the frequencies for 26, 27, 28, 29, and 30 "believers," and then dividing by 100. The theoretical probability is approximately 0.26.

Use after page 528.

Unit 7

In-Class Exam

You will need a table of random digits or your calculator.

1. A Retired Police Officers' Organization has an annual fund-raising drive in which tickets to a benefits concert are sold by telephone. From past experience, the director of the fund-raising drive knows that about 25% of telephone calls result in the sale of at least one ticket. The director would like to estimate the average number of phone calls needed before a sale is made.

   a. Describe a simulation model of the number of phone calls made by the Retired Police Officers' Organization before a ticket sale is made.

   b. Run your simulation 5 times. Add your results to the frequency table below so that there is a total of 100 trials. Use the "Frequency (After)" column to record the final results.

Number of Call of First Sale	Frequency (Before)	Frequency (After)	Number of Call of First Sale	Frequency (Before)	Frequency (After)
1	28		9	2	
2	15		10	2	
3	16		11	0	
4	9		12	1	
5	7		13	1	
6	5		14	0	
7	4		15	0	
8	4		16	1	
			Total	95	100

   c. Using this frequency table, what is the average number of the call of the first sale? Explain how you obtained your response.

   Average number: _____

   Explanation:

In-Class Exam

2. **a.** Describe a simulation model for the situation in which parents may have up to two children, but only one female child.

b. Run the simulation 10 times, and record the results in the frequency table below.

Children	Frequency
G	
BG	
BB	
Total	10

c. Using your results in Part b, find the percentage of male and female children.

Females: _____   *Males:* _____

3. Suppose a recent survey found that 70% of adults believed their local school was doing a good job of educating its students.

a. Assuming this is true, describe how to use a random digit table or calculator to simulate whether a randomly chosen adult believes the local school is doing a good job.

In-Class Exam

b. Describe how to use your simulation to see how many in a random sample of 30 adults believe their local school is doing a good job.

c. Perform 5 trials of your simulation in Part b. Add your results to the frequencies below using the "Frequency (After)" column. The total will be 100 trials.

Number Who Think Local School Doing Good Job	Frequency (Before)	Frequency (After)
16	1	
17	2	
18	4	
19	5	
20	10	
21	11	
22	19	
23	17	
24	14	
25	8	
26	4	
27	0	
28	0	
29	0	
30	0	
Total	95	100

d. Using the data in Part c, estimate the probability that more than 25 out of 30 adults who are asked will think that their local school is doing a good job.

Probability: _____

Suggested Solutions

1. **a.** Using a table of random digits, one way is to let 0 and 1 mean a sale, 2, 3, 4, 5, 6, and 7 mean no sale, and ignore 8 and 9. Using the calculator command "int 4 rand", let 0 represent a sale and 1, 2, and 3 represent no sale. If a call results in no sale, try again and keep track of the number of calls needed until a sale is made. When a sale is made, stop, record the number of the call on which the sale is made, and then start over.

   b. The results will depend on the outcomes of the students' trials.

   c. The results will depend on the outcomes of the students' trials. To find the average, multiply each call number of the first sale by its frequency, and add these. Divide the sum by 100. The theoretical average is 4.

2. **a.** Using a table of random digits or the calculator command "int 2 rand + 1", one way is to let odd digits represent a male and even digits represent a female. Find the gender of the first child in a family. If the first child is a girl, stop, record this in a table, and start over. If the first child is a boy, try again. Record BB or BG depending on whether the second child is a boy or girl, and then start over.

   b. The results will depend on the outcomes of the students' trials.

   c. The results will depend on the outcomes of the students' trials. To find the percentage of female children, evaluate the following expression:

   $$\frac{\text{Frequency of BG} + 2 \cdot \text{Frequency of BB}}{\text{Frequency of G} + 2 \cdot \text{Frequency of BG} + 2 \cdot \text{Frequency of BB}}$$

   The percent of female children will be 100% – (*percent of male children*). The theoretical percentages are 50% for each.

3. **a.** Using a table of random digits or the calculator command "int 10 rand", one way is to let 0 through 6 mean that a person believes the local school is doing a good job and 7, 8, and 9 mean that person does not believe this.

   b. Repeat the simulation in Part a 30 times, and record the number of "believers" in those 30. Start over and repeat this process often enough to get a good estimate.

   c. The results will depend on the outcomes of the students' trials.

   d. The results depend on the outcomes of the students' trials. The probability can be estimated by adding the frequencies for 26, 27, 28, 29, and 30 "believers," and then dividing by 100. The theoretical probability is approximately 0.030.

Take-Home Assessment

1. Use the kinds of situations that were simulated in this unit as a basis for developing a simulation model of a situation of interest to you. For example, sports (using baseball players' batting averages and other statistics, for example, to simulate a team's performance) is an area in which simulations can be interesting. Write a report in which you give the background of the situation you choose, describe the simulation, and outline your assumptions. Give the results after an appropriate number of trials, explain why you think this is an appropriate number of trials, and discuss the meaning of your findings in the situation that you simulated.

2. There are computer programs and computer languages that can simulate more complicated situations than those you studied in this unit. In your library, find a book or magazine article or two on computer simulations that are of interest to you. Write a report that describes how the simulations work, how they use random number generation, the kinds of problems that can be solved with these simulations, and how people make use of the results of the simulations.

3. Write in your own words the meaning of the Law of Large Numbers. Illustrate it by completing varying numbers of trials using coins, dice, or other random number generators. Organize your writing and the data from your examples into a short report.

Unit 7

1. This project may be done individually or by pairs of students. Many popular games such as the game of Life and Monopoly purport to be simulations. The game of Life is one that is quite complex. There are many versions of simulated baseball, football, basketball, and other sports which are designed so that simulated professional athletes perform at about the same level as their real-life statistics. Other simulations involve landing space crafts, planning and making investments, and managing various complex activities. Your students may want to examine a game like one of the above to see if its assumptions are realistic. Their own projects could be simplified versions of these.

2. This project may be of particular interest to students who enjoy working with computers. The suggestion given in the comments on the previous item apply here, too. Many of the simulations described above are computerized or at least available in computer versions. The topic of computer simulations can be powerfully seductive for some students, especially if the situation being simulated is one of great interest to them.

3. The Law of Large Numbers says, essentially, that the outcomes of more and more trials of a simulation approach the theoretical probabilities inherent in the situation. This is the key idea underlying empirical probability. Students should toss a coin hundreds of times to watch the ratio of heads or tails to number of tosses approach 0.5, or roll a die and watch the ratio of any outcome to number of rolls approach $\frac{1}{6}$.

Project

Simulating for All

Purpose

In this unit you have completed many simulations. In this project you will explain to others how simulations work and what their results mean. By organizing your own thinking about simulation and observing how others respond to your instruction, you should come to a more complete understanding of randomness and simulation.

Directions

1. Imagine yourselves as mathematics teachers who are planning a team-taught lesson on random numbers and simulation. Before beginning to plan, you should have an audience in mind. Each member of your group should select a "student" from friends or family members who are not studying, and has not studied, mathematics using your textbook.

2. Describe your student to other group members. Include that student's relationship to you, math background and interests, experience with a graphing calculator or computer (if any), and any other characteristics that might have a bearing on how the lesson should be planned.

3. After all "students" are identified, decide as a group whether the lesson will be taught to students individually or as a group. This decision will also affect your planning.

4. When the teaching conditions are all decided, develop a short lesson (15–20 minutes). The lesson is to explain what random numbers are and how they are used, demonstrate how to generate them on a calculator or computer, and have the students work through a simulation or exercise to demonstrate that they can use the random numbers they generated. If possible, present the lesson to your group's "students." Then collect their work and give them feedback on how they did.

5. Write a report that includes the details of your lesson, your students' work, a paragraph about what students learned, and a description of what you would change in your lesson if you were to do it again.

Simulating for All

"People learn best from teaching others." This project is an attempt to put this old educational adage into practice. Practicing the calculator procedures for generating random numbers that meet various conditions is helpful. However, much more powerful learning will result from actually thinking through how to teach someone these procedures, then carrying out the teaching plan, and finally reflecting on how well the plan worked and how it might be improved. Rather than teaching a group of family members or friends outside of school, it may be possible for you to arrange for your students to teach another class in school.

Suggested Timeline

Give students two or three days to identify and share information about their intended "students." Allow another week for them to plan the lesson. When they have a draft lesson plan ready, have them submit it for your feedback and allow a day or so for them to respond to your feedback, depending on how extensive it is. The groups should schedule their teaching over a few days and then have a week to write their reports. You may want students to submit a draft of their report to you before they finalize it.

Suggested Report Format

Guidelines for your students might be similar to the following.

Your first task is to introduce to the reader your "students," the "classroom setting," and the lesson. When describing your lesson, provide enough detail so that someone else could teach the same lesson. Be sure to explain why you organized the lesson in the manner that you did. Your report should also include a description of how the lesson actually worked, including all "students'" work. Finally, reflect on your lesson and discuss its strengths, weaknesses, and any needed revisions.

Suggested Evaluation Criteria

1.	The format of the report follows directions.	20%
2.	Quality and completeness of the lesson plan	40%
3.	Appropriateness of the plan and its execution for target students	20%
4.	Quality of analysis of strengths, weaknesses, and needed revisions	20%

Project

Keep the Line Moving

Purpose

In this unit, you have completed many simulations. This project is a simulation of a common situation involving queuing, or the probability theory of waiting in (or on) line. Service businesses, such as banks or grocery stores, are faced every day with the issue of how many lines to have open in order to serve customers in a timely fashion during busy times, yet keep the expense of hiring employees at a minimum.

Directions

1. Suppose your group manages an ice-cream vending booth in the arena where a local team plays basketball. You would like to simulate the situation of a single server and customers waiting in line to be served. Make the following assumptions:

   a. The server can handle five customers per minute on the average.

   b. During average business times, it is equally likely that from 0 to 9 customers will get in this server's line during each minute.

   c. During busy times, it is equally likely that 5 to 15 customers will get in this server's line during each minute.

2. Describe how to use a random number generator to simulate, for this server, a typical 15-minute period during average times and a 15-minute period during busy times.

3. Run each simulation at least 500 times and record (a) the number of people in line at the end of each minute, (b) the length of time the server had no customers, and (c) the length of time each customer had to wait to be served.

4. Write a report of your project. Include a careful description of the simulation model you used with an explanation of why it is appropriate each part and the number of times you conducted it to generate your data. Describe your findings including the mean of each part of Task 3 above for average times and for busy times. Explain how the information could be useful to you as the manager of the booth.

Keep the Line Moving

This activity should be done by a group of students. It will probably require a great deal of group discussion and guidance from you for all students to understand what is going on here. Walk students through the steps of the activity of standing in line, getting served, and so forth, following the time assumptions given in the statement of the problem. The simulation will require randomly generating the number of customers who show up in each of 15 consecutive minutes and noting how many are in line at the end of each minute. It would be especially interesting for students to design and carry out the simulation, and then gather real data from a concession stand at a sporting event, to see if the assumptions are realistic. It may take longer in real life to serve a customer, or they may come in very uneven numbers. The assumptions can then be adjusted to fit the real data more accurately.

Suggested Timeline

Give students ample time to be sure they all understand the problem. Allow a few days for them to design their simulation. When they have a simulation designed, have them submit it for your feedback and allow a day or so for them to respond to your feedback, depending on how extensive it is. Allow a week for them to conduct the simulation trials and to write their report. You may want them to submit a draft of the report to you before it is finalized.

Report Format

Guidelines for your students might be similar to the following.

The introduction to your report should introduce the reader to the situation that you are going to simulate and should include some reasons why someone might want to know the results of your simulation. You should clearly describe your simulation model and why it is accurate. In the presentation of your findings, be sure to include an organized display of the results of your 500 trials for both typical and busy times. Think about how best to display these data. The summary of your data should include the mean number of people in line at the end of each minute, the mean length of time the server had no customers, and the mean length of time each customer had to wait. Finally, be sure that your report explains how the information could be useful to you as the manager of the booth.

Suggested Evaluation Criteria

1. The format of the report follows directions.   20%
2. Accuracy of the simulation model   40%
3. Quality and completeness of the report of simulation results   20%
4. Quality of analysis of findings for the concession stand manager   20%

Unit 7

Since procedures and time frames for final examinations vary so much from school to school, we provide a variety of assessment tasks from which you may choose. You should choose tasks and construct an exam that fit your particular class needs and emphases. To help you choose, a brief summary of the tasks follows.

1. This task asks students to describe a distribution, discuss the effect of eliminating an outlier on the mean and median, and describe a measure of variability for the data set. (**Unit 1**)

2. This task assesses understanding of important statistical ideas, including mean, median, mode, mean absolute deviation, box plots, and histograms. (**Unit 1**)

3. This task is a variation on the bungee-jump investigation that students completed in Unit 2. In this case, a two-passenger cage is suspended on bungee cords hooked between two towers. The cage is then pulled to the ground, so that when released it will be projected rapidly upward. Students are given the graph of height versus time for the cage's motion and asked to analyze its motion and note its position at various times. (**Unit 2**)

4. This task is an application involving a linear function. It measures understanding of the connection between the application and the function that models it and the ability to solve for one variable in an equation when the value of the other is given. (**Unit 3**)

5. This task requires students to solve some simple linear equations, show their work, and explain how to check the solution. (**Unit 3**)

6. This task is another application involving a linear function, but this one starts with a graph. It measures students' ability to interpret a graph, find an equation given the graph, and apply the equation to the real-world situation. (**Unit 3**)

7. This task assesses whether students can simplify a linear expression involving the distributive property. In addition, students must explain why they are sure their simplified equation is equivalent to the given one. (**Unit 3**)

8. This task requires students to match, with reasons, each of two given real-world problems to the graph model (Euler circuits or paths, graph coloring, or critical paths) that fits it. (**Unit 4**)

9. This task is an application that can be modeled with a vertex-edge graph. Students sketch a graph representing a verbally described situation, sketch a path that meets certain given conditions, determine whether or not their graph has an Euler circuit, and finally Eulerize the graph. (**Unit 4**)

10. This task requires students to use a digraph analysis to find the critical path and the earliest finish time to complete a complex task, when task time and immediate prerequisites are given for each task. (**Unit 4**)

Units 1–7

11. This task assesses students' ability to sketch three-dimensional boxes from given two-dimensional nets and to find the volume, surface area, and symmetry planes of the boxes. (**Unit 5**)

12. This task assesses some of the same ideas as Task 11, but in different ways. It requires students to make a three-dimensional sketch of a box, find the length of a diagonal of a face, sketch the symmetry planes, sketch a net that could be a pattern for the box, and compute the volume and surface area. (**Unit 5**)

13. This task is an application that requires students to sketch cylinders (cans) packed in a box and then to apply area and volume ideas for the cylinder and the box. (**Unit 5**)

14. This task assesses students' understanding of exponents and their properties. Beyond computing with exponents, students need to explain their reasoning about the exponential expressions. (**Unit 6**)

15. This task is an application involving exponential models. Given information about present population and the percent of annual growth, students complete a table of estimated population in future years, write both a *NOW-NEXT* and a "$y = \ldots$" equation that model the growth, and use their equations to make a prediction. (**Unit 6**)

16. This task requires students to examine the effect of a credit card's monthly service charge on an unpaid balance over several months. Students construct a table of monthly balances and a graph of the same data. They then write a *NOW-NEXT* equation that models the monthly growth in the balance and use it to compute the result of variations in the beginning balance and in the rate of the monthly service charge. (**Unit 6**)

17. This task requires students to describe a simulation model for a probabilistic situation, conduct a few trials of the simulation, estimate an empirical probability from a simulation table, and describe the effects of increasing the sample size. (**Unit 7**)

18. This task is an application involving both linear and exponential models. Given data over time, students plot it and decide what type of model is needed. They then find a model and use it to make predictions. Original data suggest an exponential model, but students need to adjust their prediction when additional data change the shape of the data set. (**Units 1, 2, 3, 6**)

19. This task requires students to compute areas of a rectangle, parallelogram, and right triangle and to use the Pythagorean Theorem to find lengths. They also make a graph model and find an Euler circuit for that model. Finally, they are required to design simulation models for two different situations and to show their understanding of the implications of the Law of Large Numbers. (**Units 4, 5, 6, 7**)

Use after page 545.

Units 1–7 Exam Tasks

Final Exam

1. Below is a histogram of the populations (in thousands) of the 40 largest cities in the United States, according to the 1990 census.

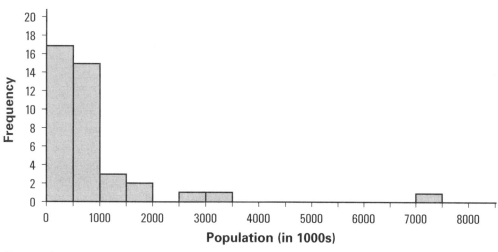

**Populations of the 40 Largest Cities
in the United States in 1990**

Source: U.S. Bureau of the Census, *Statistical Abstract of the United States: 1991* (111th edition). Washington, D.C., 1991.

a. How many of these cities had populations of less than 1,000,000?

Number of cities: _____

b. Describe the distribution of the populations of the 40 largest cities in the United States in 1990.

c. Estimate the median of the data set. Explain your process for estimating the median.

Estimate of median: _____

Explanation:

Units 1–7

Units 1–7 Exam Tasks

d. Would you expect the median to be larger, the same, or smaller than the mean? Explain your response.

Larger _____   *The same* _____   *Smaller* _____
Explanation:

e. New York had a population of 7,323,000 in 1990. Suppose the population of New York was deleted from this data set and a new mean and median were computed. How would the new mean and median compare to the original mean and median?

f. Populations (in millions) of three large cities are plotted below as a function of time.

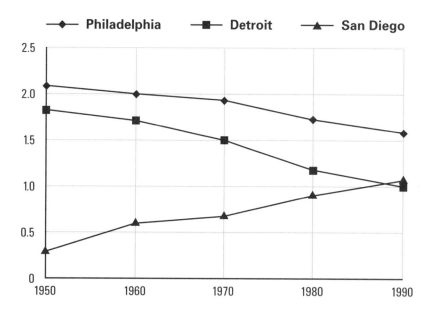

Describe and compare the changes in population of these three cities over this 40-year span.

Use after page 545.

Units 1–7 Exam Tasks

2. This task assesses your proficiency with and understanding of some important techniques for summarizing and exploring data sets.

   a. The histogram for a distribution has the following shape.

   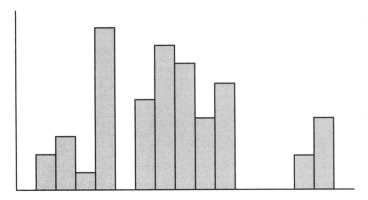

   Indicate the order, from smallest to largest, of the mean, median, and mode of this distribution. Explain your reasoning.

   Order from smallest to largest: _____

   Explanation:

   b. Compute the mean absolute deviation (MAD) of the following set of data: 5, 7, 9, 12, 17. Show or explain your work.

   Mean absolute deviation: _____

   Work or explanation:

   c. Describe the kinds of information you can get about a distribution by examining its (i) box plot and (ii) histogram.

   i. box plot: *ii. histogram:*

   d. Describe the kinds of situations for which a box plot is more useful than a histogram and for which a histogram is more useful than a box plot.

Units 1 – 7

Units 1–7 Exam Tasks

Final Exam

3. At Olde Towne Mall, near Orlando, Florida, there is a carnival ride called "The Human Slingshot." A two-passenger cage is suspended on very strong bungee cords and hooked between two tall towers, as shown on the left below. The cage is pulled to the ground and released. In one test of this apparatus, a radar gun was used to study the path of the cage after a test release. The radar was connected directly to a computer that produced a graph of the cage's motion.

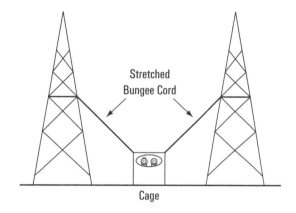

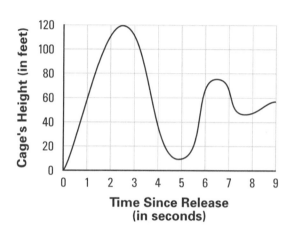

a. What does the pattern of the graph tell you about the cage's motion?

b. According to the graph, what was the approximate height above the ground one second after the release of the cage, two seconds after release, and four seconds after release?

   After 1 second: _____   *After 2 seconds:* _____

   After 4 seconds: _____

c. After the first second of the test, when did the cage come closest to the ground? How close to the ground was the cage?

   Time when closest to ground: _____   *Closest distance to ground:* _____

d. When did the cage reach its highest point? How high was that?

   Time when at highest point: _____   *Greatest height:* _____

Units 1–7 Exam Tasks

4. The number of gallons y of gasoline left in a large motorboat after traveling x miles since filling the tank is given by

$$y = 20 - 0.2x$$

a. Explain what 20 and -0.2 in the equation tell about the relation between miles traveled and gasoline left.

b. Graph the equation. Explain the role of 30 and -0.2 in the graph.

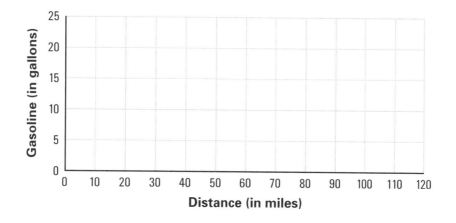

Units 1 – 7

Units 1–7 Exam Tasks

c. After filling the gasoline tank, Helen drove the boat until there were 10 gallons left. How many miles had she driven? Explain how you can tell from the equation and how you can tell from the graph.

Miles driven: _____

Explanation:

d. When Helen has filled the boat's tank, how many miles can she go before refueling? Show or explain your work.

Maximum miles: _____

Explanation:

5. Solve these equations. Show or explain both your work and how to check each solution.

a. $126 = 84 - 14x$

Work:

Check:

Solution: _____

b. $5x + 20 = 36$

Work:

Check:

Solution: _____

Units 1–7 Exam Tasks

Final Exam

6. The California Gold Rush of 1849 caused rapid increase in the populations of towns in the area for the next decade. Suppose the graph below shows the population growth of Sutterville from year 0 (the end of 1849) to 10 (the end of 1859).

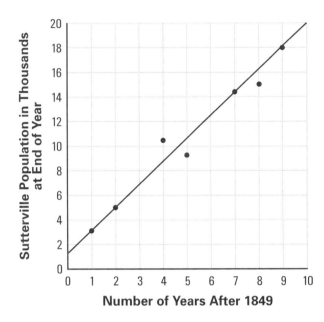

Number of Years After 1849

a. Use the line from the graph model to answer the following questions.

■ James Buchanan was elected president in 1856. What was Sutterville's population at the end of that year?

Population: _____

■ When a city's population reached 6,000, it was assigned a United States marshal. When did this happen in Sutterville?

Year: _____

■ What was Sutterville's approximate population at the end of 1849?

Population: _____

■ About how much did Sutterville's population increase during 1850? By about how much do you expect it to have increased during 1859?

1850 population increase: _____   *1859 population increase:* _____

Units 1–7

Units 1–7 Exam Tasks

b. Find an equation for this linear population growth model. Explain your method.

Equation: _____

Explanation:

c. Show how to use your equation in Part b to answer each of the first two questions in Part a. Explain or show your work. The answers should be very nearly the same as those you gave in Part a.

▪ Buchanan question

▪ U.S. marshal question

Population: _____

Year: _____

7. For the equation $y = 52 + 20(x - 4)$, write an equivalent equation in the form $y = a + bx$. Explain how you are sure that the new equation is equivalent to the given one.

Equation: _____

Explanation:

Units 1–7 Exam Tasks

8. You studied three graph models in Unit 4:

   i. Euler circuits and paths

   ii. graph coloring

   iii. critical paths

   For Parts a and b, indicate which graph model you would use to model the problem, what the vertices and edges would represent, and explain why you chose the graph model you did.

   a. Karen delivers papers to all the houses along the streets in a certain part of town. Each morning she leaves her house, which is at a street corner, delivers the papers so that she does not travel any street more than once, and ends at her friend Gina's house at another street corner. The problem is to find a route that Karen can take.

   Model needed (check one)   i ____   ii ____   iii ____

   Vertices represent _____

   Edges represent _____

   Explanation:

   b. A building contractor is planning to restore a historic mansion. He has made a list of 15 tasks that need to be completed. He also has recorded the length of time each task takes and the prerequisites for each task. The problem is to plan the entire job in order to minimize the length of time it will take.

   Model needed (check one)   i ____   ii ____   iii ____

   Vertices represent _____

   Edges represent _____

   Explanation:

Units 1–7

Units 1–7 Exam Tasks

c. The problems in Parts a and b used two of the three graph models. Give an example of a problem that can be solved using the third graph model, that is, the one that was not needed for Part a or for Part b. Indicate what the vertices and edges would represent in your problem, and explain your answer.

Example problem:

Vertices represent _____

Edges represent _____

Explanation:

Use after page 545.

Units 1–7 Exam Tasks

9. Elijah delivers papers to all the houses along the streets in a four-block area of town (shown in the map on the right). He wants to start at his house, which is at street corner *K*, deliver the papers so that he does not travel any street more than once, and end at his friend's house at street corner *G*. Where there are houses on both sides of the street, papers must be delivered to both sides by going along one side and then the other.

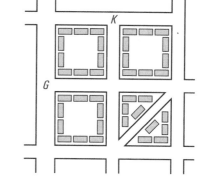

a. Sketch a graph model for this situation, labeling all vertices with single-letter labels. Is it possible for Elijah to start at his house and end at his friend's house without traveling any street twice? Explain how you know from the graph model.

Possible _____   *Not possible* _____

Explanation:

b. Does your graph have an Euler circuit? If so, use your vertex labels to describe the circuit. If not, explain why not, and explain how to Eulerize your graph.

Units 1–7 Exam Tasks

10. A building contractor is planning to restore a historic mansion. Nine tasks that need to be completed, the length of time each task takes, and the prerequisites for each task are given in the table below. The contractor wants to plan the entire job in order to minimize the length of time it will take. Draw the digraph for this job, mark the critical path, and find the earliest finish time (EFT) for the whole project.

Task	Task Time	Immediate Prerequisite
Prepare Blueprints of the Restoration (B)	3 days	none
Remove Old Flooring (F)	4 days	B
Replace Water Damaged Supports (W)	0.5 days	F
Remove Damaged Siding (R)	2 days	none
Electrical Work (E)	8 days	W
Plumbing Work (P)	6 days	W
Complete Exterior Work (Ex)	13 days	R
Complete Interior Work (I)	10 days	E, P
Landscaping (L)	7 days	Ex

Units 1–7 Exam Tasks

11. Boxes of various shapes are required to package farm equipment. Shown at the right is the net for one box used to package sections of a hog feeder.

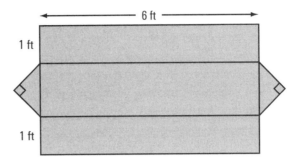

a. Make a sketch of the assembled, three-dimensional box.

b. Sketch all symmetry planes of the box. Explain how these are related to the symmetries of its faces.

c. Sketch one other possible net that could be used to manufacture the same box.

d. Find the volume and surface area of the box. Show or explain your work.

Volume (units): _____   *Surface area (units):* _____

12. The Quintana family bought a grandfather clock to put in the entryway. It came in a rectangular box whose dimensions were 18 inches by 24 inches by 6 feet.

    a. Make a sketch of the three-dimensional box. Label all of the lengths of the edges. Find the length of the longest diagonal of a face of the box.

    b. Sketch all symmetry planes of the box. Explain how these are related to the symmetries of its faces.

    c. Sketch a net that could be used as a pattern for the manufacture of the box.

    d. Find the volume of the box expressed in cubic feet and the surface area of the box expressed in square feet. Show or explain your work.

        Volume: _____   *Surface area:* _____

        Explanation or work:

Units 1–7 Exam Tasks

13. Cans of peaches are placed upright in a shipping box in two snugly packed layers. Each layer contains 3 rows of cans with 4 cans per row. For each question below, show your work and give the appropriate units for your numerical answers.

a. When the box is opened by cutting off the top, the tops of the first layer of cans are all that is visible. Make a sketch of how this would look from directly above the box.

b. If the diameter of the base of each can is 7.5 cm, find the smallest possible dimensions of the rectangular top. Explain.

Smallest dimensions: _____

Explanation:

c. If the height of each can is 11 cm, find the smallest possible height of the box. Explain.

Smallest height: _____

Explanation:

d. Using the can's dimensions given in Parts b and c, find the volume of the smallest shipping box possible.

Volume of smallest box: _____

Units 1 – 7

e. Because the cans are cylindrical and the box is a rectangular prism, there will be space between packed cans. Determine the total amount of such space in the smallest possible box. Explain your method for finding this volume.

Space between cans: _____

Explanation:

f. Determine the amount of cardboard required to make a shipping box of the smallest possible dimensions, including top, bottom, and all sides. (Ignore the amount due to overlap, since that will vary.)

Amount of cardboard: _____

g. A paper label covers the entire curved surface of each can of peaches. Determine the least amount of paper required to make one of these labels. (Ignore the amount due to overlap, since that will vary.)

Amount of paper: _____

Units 1–7 Exam Tasks

14. a. If $2^3 = 8$, $2^5 = 32$, and $(8)(32) = 2^n$, then $n =$ _____. Explain how you know this.

Explanation:

b. ■ Find $3(2^x)$ if $x = 4$. _____

■ Are $3(2^x)$ and 6^x equivalent for all x? Explain.

Yes ____   *No* ____

Explanation:

15. *The World Almanac and Book of Facts, 1996*, reports that the 1990 population of Australia was about 18.3 million people. The annual rate of growth is estimated at 1%.

a. Make a table showing the estimated population of Australia, to the nearest tenth of a million, for each year from 1991 to 1996.

Year	1991	1992	1993	1994	1995	1996
Estimated Population						

b. Write a *NOW-NEXT* equation that could be used to calculate Australia's population estimate for any year based on the previous year's population.

c. Write an equation of the form "$y = \ldots$" that could be used to calculate population estimates for Australia at any time after 1990.

d. Use the equation in Part b or c to estimate the population of Australia in 2010. Explain how you arrived at your estimate.

Units 1 – 7

Units 1–7 Exam Tasks

Final Exam

16. As the end of the year gets close, many department and appliance stores have special payment plans available. Maurice spent $5,000 on a home entertainment system under a plan that charged no interest for twelve months, so for twelve months he paid no money. When his first bill arrived, he discovered the "catch" to the plan: the debt would be interest free only if he paid it all before the twelve months had passed. Since he hadn't paid anything, he also owed all the interest that normally would have been added over those twelve months, at a rate of 1.4% per month.

   a. Make a table showing the debt, with interest, for each month.

Month	Balance		Month	Balance
0	$5000		7	
1			8	
2			9	
3			10	
4			11	
5			12	
6				

   b. Mark a scale on the vertical axis, and graph the data in your table in Part a.

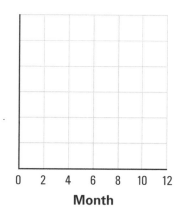

Use after page 545.

c. Write *NOW-NEXT* and exponential equations that could be used to calculate the amount Maurice would owe each month for a large number of months. Explain how you found your equations.

NEXT = _____ y = _____

Explanation: *Explanation:*

d. Find the balance that Maurice would owe after 12 months if he spent $8,000. Show or explain your work.

Balance after 12 months: _____

Work or explanation:

e. Find the balance Maurice would owe after 12 months if the interest was 1% per month, and he spent $5,000. Show or explain your work.

Balance after 12 months: _____

Work or explanation:

Units 1–7

Units 1–7 Exam Tasks

17. Eighty percent of the high school students in a large district passed a physical fitness test and twenty percent failed. The supervisor decides to choose random students from the school district to find out what they do for physical fitness.

a. Describe one trial of a simulation that can be used to approximate the probability that in a randomly selected sample of 10 students, there would be no students who failed the physical fitness test. Your simulation model should use the random number function of your calculator or computer software or a table of random digits.

b. Conduct five trials of your simulation and add the results to the frequency table below so that there is a total of 200 trials.

Number Who Failed the Fitness Test	Frequency Before Five Trials	Frequency After Five Trials
0	21	
1	54	
2	57	
3	39	
4	18	
5	5	
6	1	
Total	195	200

c. What is your estimate of the probability that a randomly selected sample of 10 students would contain no one who failed the physical fitness test?

Estimate of probability: _____

d. What will happen to the percentage of students in the sample who failed if the sample size is increased to 16 students?

Use after page 545.

Units 1–7 Exam Tasks

Final Exam

18. The data given in this task are from the *HIV/AIDS Surveillance Report.*

Number of New AIDS Cases by Year

Year	1981	1982	1983	1984	1985	1986	1987
Children under 13	16	29	75	112	228	325	480

Source: U.S. Department of Health and Human Services, *HIV/AIDS Surveillance Report 5, No. 2* (July 1993).

  a. Make an appropriate plot showing how the number of new AIDS cases among children under 13 changed over time from 1981 to 1987.

  b. Write a brief description of the pattern of change in the number of new cases of AIDS among children under 13 from 1981 to 1987.

  c. Based on the data above, would a linear model or an exponential model be likely to help you make the best prediction of the number of new AIDS cases among children under 13 in the year 2000? Explain your reasoning.

  Linear model: _____   *Exponential model:* _____

  Explanation:

d. Find a linear model and an exponential model for the data. Use 1–7 for the years instead of 1981–1987 when you do the calculation. Explain your work.

Linear model: _____   *Exponential model:* _____

Explanation:

e. Use each model to predict the number of new AIDS cases among children under 13 in the year 2000. Explain your work.

Linear prediction: _____   *Exponential prediction:* _____

Explanation:

f. Given the following additional data, how would you adjust your predictions in Part e? Explain your reasoning and show your work.

Number of New AIDS Cases by Year

Year	1988	1989	1990	1991	1992
Children under 13	597	684	730	652	649

Source: U.S. Department of Health and Human Services, *HIV/AIDS Surveillance Report 5, No. 2* (July 1993).

Adjusted prediction: _____

Explanation and work:

Units 1–7 Exam Tasks

Final Exam

19. The junior class of Davison High School is sponsoring a fruit sale to raise money for their senior class trip next year. Ten students who live in the same residential district have divided the district into 10 regions of approximately equal area. Each of the students agrees on a region in which she or he is to go to each house in an attempt to sell some of the fruit. A map of Renee's region is shown here.

   a. The three blocks in Renee's region are in the shape of a rectangle, a right triangle, and a parallelogram. The rectangle is 0.2 miles long and 0.1 mile wide. The height (longer leg) of the right triangular block is 0.1 mile and its base (shorter leg) is 0.05 miles. The parallelogram block's height is the same as that of the right triangle, and its base is the same as the length of the rectangle, as the map indicates. If the area of Renee's region is average for the 10 regions, what is the approximate area of the residential district? Explain or show your work.

   b. Renee wants to be as efficient as possible when she visits the houses in her region. Make a graph model of Renee's region, assuming that as she goes down a street she stops at the houses on one side only. Explain what the vertices and edges represent in your model.

c. Use a method you learned in the "Graph Models" unit to find an efficient order for Renee to visit the houses so that she does not have to go past houses that she has already visited, if that is possible. If it is not possible, explain why not, and find a route that has as little backtracking as possible.

d. Find the distance in miles that Renee will need to travel to go from the first house to the last house using the order you proposed in Part c. Explain or show your work.

Distance: _____

Explanation or work:

e. The company that is providing the fruit for the sale has a great deal of experience with such sales. They estimate that a sale will result from 25% of the house calls. Assume this is the probability for the Davison juniors.

   The number of houses on a block varies greatly. For example, there are 4 houses on the triangular block in Renee's region and 16 on each of the larger blocks. Do you think the number of houses on a block affects the chances that no sales are made on that block? If so, do you think this is more likely to happen on larger blocks or on smaller ones? Explain your reasoning.

Use after page 545.

Units 1 – 7

f. Describe two related simulation models to find the number of sales that are made on a block. In the first case, the block has just 4 houses, and in the second case, the block has 16 houses. Write instructions for performing one trial of each simulation model.

g. Conduct 15 trials of each simulation to test the conjecture you made in Part e. Make a histogram of your results.

h. Are the results of your simulations different from your conjecture in Part e? What should you conclude about how the number of houses on a block affects the chances of no sales on the block, and why?

Units 1 – 7

Suggested Solutions

1. **a.** Thirty-two of these cities had populations of less than 1,000,000, as seen in the first two bars of the histogram.

    b. The distribution of populations in the 40 largest cities is skewed to the right. There is one city that has a population between 7,000,000 and 7,500,000. This population is much larger than that of the other cities, making it an outlier. Only eight of the cities have populations that are 1,000,000 or larger.

    c. The median will be the average of the 20th and 21st populations. Since 17 data values are less than 500,000 and 15 are between 500,000 and 1,000,000, we know that the median will be between 500,000 and 1,000,000.

    d. We expect the median of the data set will be smaller than the mean since this is typical of data that are skewed right. The outlier will have an effect on the mean, but not on the median.

    e. The new median would probably be very close to the old one. However, since the 7,323,000 was an outlier, removing it from the data set will affect the mean. The new mean will be less than the old mean and the difference between the two probably will be fairly large.

    f. Philadelphia's population has steadily decreased, at the rate of a little over 100,000 each 10 years. Detroit's population has decreased, too, but more rapidly since 1960 than in the 1950s. San Diego's population, on the other hand, increased at a fairly steady rate of about 200,000 in each 10-year period from 1950 to 1990.

2. **a.** The mode is smallest, then the median, and the mean is largest. The mode is the tallest bar, which clearly occurs at a point on the x-axis that is below the median, which is the point at which half the data points are above and half are below. The mean, but not the median or mode, will be pulled upward by the existence of the data points on the far right.

    b. The mean of these 5 data points is 10. The MAD is the average of the absolute values of the deviations from 10.

    $$\text{MAD} = \frac{5+3+1+2+7}{5} = 3.6$$

    c. A box plot shows the minimum, each quartile, and the maximum. A histogram shows the frequency of each interval of values in the distribution.

    d. A box plot is more useful for comparing many distributions when only the general locations of the distributions are to be compared (as in Organizing Task 3 on page 60 of the student text). A histogram is more useful if you want to see the details about the shape of a distribution.

 Use after page 545.

Units 1–7

Suggested Solutions (*continued*)

3. **a.** Upon release, the cage goes up rapidly and begins to slow as it approaches its first peak. It then drops, picking up speed at first, but slowing again as it reaches its first low point. It then repeats this up-and-down pattern several times, but each time the peaks are lower and the low points are higher, until the cage reaches a resting point stretched between the two towers.

   b. After 1 second, about 60 feet; after 2 seconds, about 112 feet; after 4 seconds, about 40 feet

   c. After approximately 4.8 seconds, it was about 7 feet above the ground.

   d. After nearly 2.5 seconds, it was about 120 feet above the ground.

4. **a.** The gas tank holds 20 gallons. The boat uses 0.2 gallons of gasoline for each mile it is driven.

   b.
   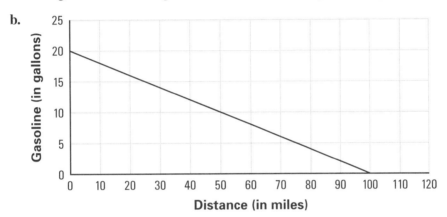

   The y-intercept of the graph or the y value when $x = 0$ is 20. The slope of the line or the rate of change in y when x increases by 1 is -0.2.

   c. 50 miles.
   In the given equation, replace y by 10 to get $10 = 20 - 0.2x$.

   Solving this equation with paper and pencil or calculator gives $x = 50$. To use the graph, locate 10 on the y-axis; then go horizontally across to the graph and find the x-coordinate of that point. The y-coordinate of the point you reach on the graph is 10 and the x-coordinate is 50. Whether you use the equation or the graph, the result indicates that when there were 10 gallons of gasoline left, Helen had driven the boat 50 miles.

   d. Helen can go 100 miles with a full tank of gas. This can be seen in the graph by noticing that when $y = 0$, then $x = 100$. Students also may determine the answer by realizing that 0.2 gallons per mile is the same as 1 gallon for 5 miles. Thus, 20 gallons will last for 20×5 or 100 miles.

Units 1–7

Suggested Solutions (*continued*)

5. **a.** $x = -3$

   Students may use a variety of methods, but they should show or explain what they do. The check can be done by substituting –3 for x in the equation or by a reasonable graphing method, such as finding the x-coordinate of the point at which $y = 84 - 14x$ intersects $y = 126$. In general, give at least some credit for any checking method that shows an understanding of the fact that –3 somehow "makes the equation true."

   b. $x = 3.2$

   The comments concerning the work and check in Part a apply here as well.

6. **a.** Answers are approximate.

   - 14,300

   - 1,852

   - 1,200

   - The increase in population was about 1,900 in both years.

   b. The approximate equation is $y = 1900x + 1200$. The values 1,900 and 1,200 are estimates from the graph. Answers to the last two questions of Part a imply that the y-intercept of the equation is 1,200 and the slope is 1,900, which leads directly to this equation. Another approach is to use two points on the graph and derive the equation from them. Good candidates are (0, 1200) and (10, 20000).

   c. For the Buchanan question, letting $x = 7$ (which corresponds to 1856) gives $y = 1900(7) + 1200$, so the population y is 14,500. For the U.S. marshal question, letting $y = 6000$, gives $6000 = 1900x + 1200$. Solving this equation for x by any of several calculator and noncalculator methods gives $x \approx 2.5$. Since 2.5 is between 2 and 3, it occurs after the end of 1851 and before the end of 1852. In other words, it is during 1852.

7. $y = 52 + 20(x - 4) = 52 + 20x - 80 = -28 + 20x$

   One explanation is to apply the distributive property in the first step and the commutative property for addition in the second step, so the expressions are equivalent at each step. Another approach is to graph the original expression and the simplified one on a graphing calculator showing that the same graph results. A third approach is to show that the equation $52 + 20(x - 4) = -28 + 20x$ reduces to $0 = 0$ and so is true for all x.

8. **a.** **i.** Euler circuits and paths

   Vertices represent street intersections, and edges represent streets on Karen's route. The goal would be to draw a vertex-edge graph that represents the map of the part of town on Karen's route. If it is possible for Karen to complete her route as described in the problem, the graph must have an Euler path that begins at Karen's house and ends at Gina's house.

© 1998 Everyday Learning Corporation

Suggested Solutions (*continued*)

   b. **iii.** critical paths

Weighted vertices would represent tasks with weights being time of completion. Directed edges would indicate immediate prerequisites, in which arrows would point from an immediate prerequisite to a task. The critical path of this directed graph would specify the order in which the tasks should be done, and the length of the critical path is the earliest finish time for the entire job.

   c. The third graph model is graph coloring. There are many possible example problems, but the key is that the problem must involve some sort of conflict, such as scheduling club meetings when a person cannot be in two meetings at once, assigning frequencies to radio stations so that nearby stations do not have the same frequency, and the classic example of coloring a map so that no two adjacent states have the same color. Typically, vertices represent the objects that may or may not be in conflict, such as states on the map, radio stations, or individual committee members, and an edge represents the existence of a conflict between the two vertices joined by the edge.

9. **a.** One graph is the following.

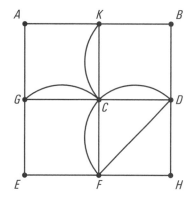

Vertices *F* and *D* are odd vertices, so it is not possible to start at *K* and end at *G*.

   b. There is no Euler circuit because there are two odd vertices. Adding a path between *F* and *D* would Eulerize the graph.

10. The critical path is indicated by the shaded vertices. The Earliest Finishing Time is 25.5 days.

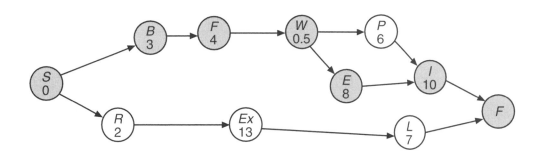

Units 1–7

Suggested Solutions (*continued*)

11. a. Here is a sketch from one perspective. There are many other possibilities.

b. There are two planes of symmetry, as pictured below. The one on the left is related to the symmetry of an isosceles triangle about the median from the vertex. The one on the right is related to the symmetry of a rectangle about a line through the midpoints of a pair of opposite sides.

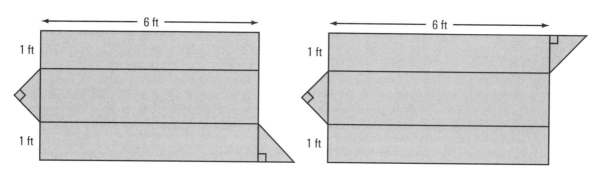

c. There are several possibilities, such as these two.

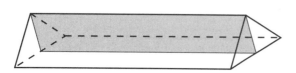 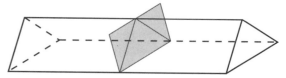

d. The volume is the area of the triangular base, $B = 0.5ab$, times the height h.

$$V = Bh = 0.5(1)(1)(6) = 3 \text{ ft}^3$$

The surface area is the sum of the areas of the two triangular bases and the three rectangular faces. The rectangle pictured in the center is 6 feet long. Its width is the hypotenuse of the triangular base, which can be found by using the Pythagorean Theorem to get $\sqrt{2}$ or about 1.414.

$$SA \approx 2(1)(6) + 2(0.5)(1)(1) + (1.414)(6) \approx 21.5 \text{ ft}^2$$

12. a. 1

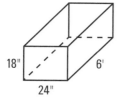

The longest diagonal is $\sqrt{2^2 + 6^2}$ or about 6.3 feet.

Suggested Solutions (*continued*)

b. There are three symmetry planes, as sketched here. The symmetry planes intersect the faces in lines of symmetries of the faces.

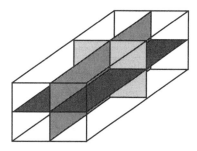

c. There are several possibilities, including the one below.

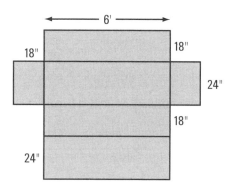

d. $V = (1.5)(2)(6) = 18$ cubic feet

$SA = 2(1.5)(2) + 2(1.5)(6) + 2(2)(6) = 48$ square feet

13. a.

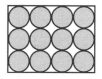

b. Width $= 3 \times 7.5 = 22.5$ cm

Length $= 4 \times 7.5 = 30$ cm

To fit the cans into the box as pictured, each dimension must be the number of cans in that dimension times the diameter of each can.

c. Since there are two layers, the box must be at least $2 \times 11 = 22$ cm in height. In reality, it would have to be a little more than that to allow for the thickness of the cardboard and of the cans' tops and bottoms.

d. The volume of the smallest possible box is $22.5 \times 30 \times 22 = 14,850$ cubic centimeters.

Suggested Solutions (*continued*)

e. The best strategy is to find the volume of each can, multiply that by 24 to get the total volume of all 24 cans, and subtract that total from the volume of the box. The volume of a can (which is a cylinder) is

$$\pi r^2 h = \pi(3.75^2)(11) \approx 486 \text{ cubic cm}$$

The total volume of all 24 cans is about 24×486 or $11,664 \text{ cm}^3$.

Finally, the volume of the space between cans is approximately $14,850 - 11,664$ or $3,186 \text{ cm}^3$.

f. The total surface area of the box required in this case is,

$$2 \times 22.5 \times 30 + 2 \times 22.5 \times 22 + 2 \times 30 \times 22 \text{ or } 3,660 \text{ cm}^2.$$

g. The lateral area of the cylindrical can is required, which is

$$\pi dh = \pi(7.5)(11) \approx 259 \text{ cm}^2$$

14. a. $n = 8$

A likely approach is to multiply $(8)(32)$ to get 256. Then using a calculator, try consecutive powers of 2 until the result is 256.

b. ■ $3(2^4) = 3(16) = 48$

■ Counterexamples like $3(2^2) = 3(4) = 12$ and $6^2 = 36$ show that these expressions are not equivalent for all x. Another approach is to show with a graphing calculator that the two expressions have different graphs.

15. a.

Year	1991	1992	1993	1994	1995	1996
Estimated Population	18.5	18.7	18.9	19.0	19.2	19.4

b. $NEXT = 1.01 \times NOW$

c. $y = 18.3(1.01)^x$

d. Using the equation in Part b, calculate the population for each year from 1990 to 2010. Using the equation in Part c, substitute 20 for x. Using either equation, the predicted population is about 22.3 million people.

16. a.

Month	Balance	Month	Balance
0	$5000	7	$5511
1	$5070	8	$5588
2	$5141	9	$5666
3	$5213	10	$5746
4	$5286	11	$5826
5	$5360	12	$5908
6	$5435		

Suggested Solutions (*continued*)

b.

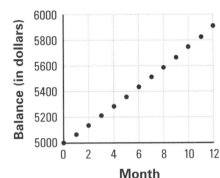

c. $NEXT = 1.014 \times NOW$

Each month the new balance is the old balance plus 1.4% of the old balance. That is equivalent to 1.014 times the old balance.

$y = 5000(1.014)^x$

The *NOW-NEXT* process means that for the *x*th month, 5000 has been multiplied by 1.014 a total of *x* times. This is the same as multiplying 5000 by 1.014^x.

d. Balance = $8000(1.014)^{12}$ = \$9452.47; The equation is the same as in Part c, except the starting point is 8000 instead of 5000.

e. Balance = $5000(1.01)^{12}$ = \$5634.13; The equation is the same as in Part c, except the rate is 1% or 0.01 instead of 1.4%.

17. a. One way to use the calculator is to enter int(10 rand) into a TI-82 (or an equivalent expression into another calculator). Pressing the ENTER key repeatedly will generate random integers from 0 to 9, inclusive. Count 0 through 7 (or any other 8 digits) as a student who passed the physical fitness test, and 8 or 9 as a student who failed. One trial will consist of examining ten digits and recording the number of 8s and 9s. To use a table of random digits, enter the table at any point and go in any direction but do not retrace. Count the digits in the same way as you would if you used your calculator as described above.

b. Responses will vary depending on the outcome of the students' simulation.

c. Students will need to use their table, so their responses may vary slightly. With the 195 trials given, the estimate from the table is $\frac{21}{195}$ or approximately 0.11. (The theoretical probability is 0.8^{10} or approximately 0.107.)

d. Students should realize that as the size of the group increases, the Law of Large Numbers indicates that the proportion of students who failed should approach 20%. So it becomes less likely that the group will not contain anybody who failed.

Units 1–7

Suggested Solutions (*continued*)

18. a.

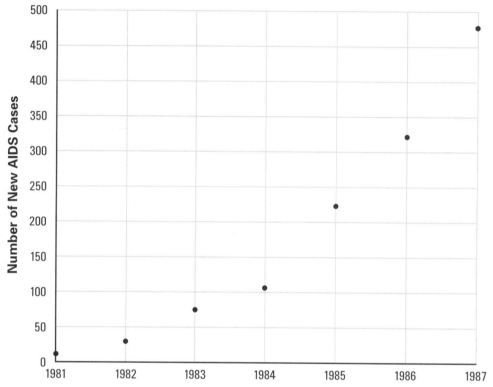

b. The number of new cases is small at first. It is increasing at an increasing rate.

c. It appears on the plot that an exponential model would be better because of the increasing rate of increase.

d. Responses may vary. For example, enter 1–7 in List 1 and the number of new cases for the corresponding year in List 2. The linear regression model is $y = 76.3x - 124.6$. The exponential regression model is $y = 10.4(1.78^x)$.

e. The year 2000 would correspond to 20; that is, 20 years after 1981. The prediction from the linear model is $76.3(20) - 124.6$ or approximately 1,401 new cases, and the prediction from the exponential model is $10.4(1.78^{20})$ or approximately 1,060,311 new cases.

f. The data from 1988 to 1992 suggest that the growth in numbers of new cases is not exponential. In fact, the number of new cases appears to have leveled off and even begun to decrease. This is probably a result of advancements in AIDS treatment and the effect of AIDS education programs. These data certainly indicate that the prediction from the exponential model is not accurate. Since it looks as though the number of cases is leveling off, a more accurate prediction from this data set might be around 650 cases. Clearly, it is difficult to predict future data because of research and education efforts.

Use after page 545.

Suggested Solutions (*continued*)

19. a. The area of Renee's region is (0.2)(0.1) + (0.2)(0.1) + (0.1)(0.05)(0.5) or 0.0425 square miles. The approximate area of the residential district is (10)(0.0425) or 0.425 square miles.

b. Vertices are street corners and edges are sides of each street with houses in Renee's region.

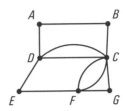

c. This graph model has an Euler circuit, since all vertices are even. An Euler circuit will be the most efficient route for Renee to follow. An example is *A-B-C-G-F-C-D-E-F-C-D-A*. There are many other possibilities.

d. The distance should be the same for all routes. The hypotenuse of the triangular block, which is equal to a slant side of the parallelogram block, can be found using the Pythagorean Theorem: $\sqrt{(0.1)^2 + (0.05)^2} \approx 0.11$.

The distance that Renee will travel is 4(0.2) + 3(0.1) + 0.05 + 3(0.11), or 1.48 miles.

e. Yes, the number of houses on a block affects the chances that no sales are made on the block. The Law of Large Numbers tells us that the more houses there are on a block, the smaller the probability is of no sales on that block.

f. One way is to key int(4 rand) + 1, or an equivalent expression, into a calculator so it will generate one of the digits 1, 2, 3, or 4 at random. Count 1 as a sale and any other number as no sale. Generate either 4 (for smaller blocks) or 16 numbers and record whether no sales are made on a block.

g. The results will vary, but after 15 trials it should be clear that the chance of no sales on a small block is much greater than the chance of no sales on a large block.

h. The answer to the first question will depend on the student's conjecture in Part e. The student should conclude that no sales on a block is more likely when there are fewer houses on the block.

Units 1–7